COUPLES
COMMUNICATION
CURE

Why Trying Harder
to Communicate Isn't Working
and What to Do Instead

MICHELE O'MARA, PHD

ISBN (Paperback): 979-8-9939435-0-3
ISBN (Ebook): 979-8-9939435-1-0

Published by Adventures in Love
9783 E 116th St PMB 3204
Fishers, Indiana 46037

ALSO BY MICHELE O'MARA, PhD

Just Ask: 1,000 Questions to Grow Your Relationship

Wholeheartedly dedicated to my love, Kristen,
the spice to my rice and the light of my life.

CONTENTS

INTRODUCTION

Do you ever feel like you and your partner speak two different languages? That no matter how hard you try, your words do not land the way you intend?

Maybe you keep repeating the same argument, hoping for a different outcome, only to feel even more misunderstood. Or perhaps the silence between you has grown so loud, you're unsure how to bridge the distance.

You're not alone. Every couple struggles with communication at some point, whether it's feeling unheard, misunderstood, or disconnected. The good news? Communication is a skill. And just like any skill, it can be learned, practiced, and mastered if you have the right tools.

That's where Wholehearted Communication comes in. You may recognize the word *wholehearted* from Brené Brown's work on Wholehearted Living. Her writing deeply influenced how many of us understand courage, vulnerability, and authenticity. What I am offering here is a practical application of that spirit, specifically for how we talk with the people we love when it matters most.

For nearly three decades, I've worked with couples who love each other but feel stuck in cycles of frustration and disconnection. Couples seek my services for many reasons: healing from betrayal, breaking free from endless conflict loops, or rediscovering the intimacy that's been replaced by routine. The ways couples drift apart are endless. The way back is not. It always begins with communication.

Surprisingly, not everyone waits until they've jumped the tracks to get help. Some couples are proactive and find a love so strong they want to shore things up right from the start, to "get it right" this time. I especially love working with these couples because they understand that no matter how strong their love is, there will be disagreements and challenges.

The question is never, "Will we disagree?" The question is always, "How will we disagree?" The answer to that question is what will make or break your relationship.

This book is for all couples. While the concepts are simple, that does not mean they are easy. There is work to be done. And realistically, that work never stops because we are in constant motion, growing, changing, and evolving.

To keep your relationship strong, you must stay aware and open to the changes happening within you, your partner, and between you. Communication is what helps us adjust and adapt as we go. It is a practice, a process of revealing your inner world with honesty while softening toward your partner in ways that let them feel safe doing the same.

With love, it always comes back to communication. Without it, love has nowhere to go. How do you express love without some form of communication? A look, a touch, a word, a gesture, even silence. Each one says something.

At its best, communication is the bridge between us. It carries emotion from one heart to another. It invites us to cross that bridge freely and often, so we remember we are not alone. We are a team. We are in this together.

Wholehearted Communication did not begin as a book. It began in 2020, when counselors' offices were overflowing and couples were buckling under the combined weight of isolation, stress, and the sudden loss of outside support systems that usually help relationships stay balanced. Like many therapists, I was at capacity. I was turning couples away who genuinely wanted help, and that did not sit well with me.

I wanted to offer something practical to the couples I could not see, something they could use on their own, without waiting months for an appointment.

In response, I began by combining the three approaches that have most strongly shaped my work, Imago Therapy, the Gottman Method, and Emotionally Focused Therapy, and translating them into an actionable, self-guided process. What began as a three-hour online class quickly proved to be too much for one sitting, so it evolved into a six-week course.

Over the next five years, I kept teaching it and revising it based on real-world feedback from couples. They told me what made sense, what helped in the moment, and what was nearly impossible to use when emotions were running high.

When couples began telling me they made more progress in weeks than they had in years of therapy, I knew this work needed a wider home. This book is the result of that process.

While this work was originally developed with lesbian couples, my primary specialty, its core principles apply to any couple willing to slow down and engage honestly. The depth of emotional awareness, communication precision, and shared power often present in these relationships offers a universal map for navigating the complexities of modern love.

I often joke that my methods were "stress-tested" in the world of lesbian relationships. If these tools can bring structure and clarity to relationships that value nuance, accountability, and emotional honesty as much as lesbian couples often do, they are sturdy enough for any couple on the planet.

How Couples Actually Use This Book

Couples come to this book in very different places.

- ▶ **Some couples begin with the self-awareness sections and never touch the scripts.** They slow down, learn to recognize their patterns, and start to understand what is happening inside them before conversations go sideways. For many, that alone changes the tone of their relationship.

- ▶ **Some couples jump straight to structure because things feel volatile.** They are tired of circular arguments, emotional blowups, or long stretches of silence, and they want something concrete to hold onto. For these couples, the scripts provide immediate containment and relief.

- ▶ **Some couples use the scripts very literally at first.** They read them word for word, stick closely to the structure, and rely on the predictability to keep conversations from escalating. Over time, the structure often loosens or becomes easier to hold. The language becomes more natural. The skills begin to show up without the scripts.

- ▶ **Some couples never use the scripts at all**, but still gain language, insight, and compassion that fundamentally shift how they relate to each other. They learn to recognize self-protection, slow themselves down, and respond with more understanding and less reactivity.

All of these are valid ways to use this book. You do not have to practice Wholehearted Communication perfectly or completely for this book to help your relationship. If you take what resonates and leave the rest, your relationship will still benefit.

Regarding the scripts themselves, it may help to think of them as training wheels. They are not meant to sound natural at first. They are meant to give you something solid to lean on when emotions are running high.

When couples are stuck in reactive patterns, their nervous systems are doing the driving. Scripts provide the scaffolding while you learn to stay present, regulated, and connected under stress. They help retrain the nervous system so that, over time, intuition replaces reactivity.

Yes, structure can feel mechanical at first. So does learning to drive. So does physical therapy. So does anything that teaches a system to move differently after it has learned to protect itself. The goal is not to rely on structure forever, but to build the capacity to respond with more choice and less reflex.

This is not a quick fix.

Wholehearted Communication is a practice. It does not work all at once. It works a little at a time. With repetition, something shifts. You start to notice what is happening while it is happening. You catch yourself sooner. You recover faster. And over time, the arguments change, or they stop showing up the way they used to.

There is no single right way to move through this book. The only requirement is a willingness to slow down and try something different together.

I.

FOUNDATIONS OF COMMUNICATION

"*People talking without speaking, people hearing without listening.*"

- PAUL SIMON, *The Sound of Silence*

CHAPTER 1

Why Communication Feels Hard and How to Make It Easier

If you've ever walked away from a conversation with your partner feeling frustrated, misunderstood, or wondering, "How did we get here?" you're not alone.

Maybe it started with, "I thought you said you were going to pick that up today?" And now it's not about dry cleaning or dog food or whatever that thing was. It's about follow-through, feeling forgotten, and why you have to keep track of everything. The task was small. The reaction? Not so much.

Sound familiar? Welcome. You're in the right place.

Communication is the lifeline of a relationship. It's how we stay close, solve problems, share love, and feel seen. And yet, for something so essential, it's surprisingly easy to fumble. That's because we're not just trading words. We're managing emotions, decoding tone, reading body language, and filtering it all through past hurts and personal histories. Add in two nervous systems that are constantly scanning for safety, and suddenly even a simple conversation can feel like a minefield. No wonder things go sideways so quickly.

At any given moment, there are three realities in play: what's happening inside you, what's happening inside your partner, and the space—the 'we'—that exists between you. Tracking all of that while trying to stay calm, clear, and connected? That's no small task.

So no, you're not failing at love. You're just human. And you're in a relationship with another human who's wired for self-protection just like you are.

This is where many couples begin to see that the issue isn't the thing they were discussing, but the communication pattern underneath it. I often hear partners say, "It was never really about the thing we were fighting about." Once you learn how to slow down and look at what's happening between you, those familiar arguments start to make more sense.

Throughout this book, you'll learn how to recognize the forks in the road. You can keep responding the way you always have or choose something new.

You can decide to take a path that is more intentional and more effective. If relationships came with a user manual, most of it would focus on understanding your nervous system and your partner's. When you learn to work with what is happening inside instead of reacting blindly against it, communication starts to flow with less struggle.

And once you learn to spot these patterns and name them, everything begins to shift. You can pause. Stay present. Reach for connection instead of control.

Wholehearted Communication: A New Approach

You don't need to be perfect to improve how you communicate.

You just need to be willing to try something different.

Wholehearted Communication offers a practical way to move beyond reactive conversations and into more intentional, connection-centered dialogue. It helps you slow things down, notice what's happening between you, and respond with more clarity instead of habit.

This is not about fixing a broken relationship. Most couples don't struggle because they don't talk. They struggle because the way they try to reach each other stops working once emotions are involved. What looks like a communication problem is often a connection problem.

Wholehearted Communication focuses on restoring connection, not just improving how you speak. That is why learning how to talk differently matters.

Real love is built through honest, sometimes uncomfortable conversations. It is shaped over time, one interaction at a time, especially when things are hard.

Wholehearted Communication is grounded in nearly thirty years of experience working with couples who want to feel more connected, understood and happy. In a world where many relationships do not last, staying connected takes more than love. It takes skill, intention, and the willingness to keep showing up.

This approach offers structure and support you can use in real conversations. It helps you stay grounded in difficult conversations and gives you tools that work when emotions are high. With practice, you will communicate with more clarity, stay emotionally connected, and move through conflict without losing each other.

What You Can Expect

This isn't a set of rigid rules or unrealistic expectations. It's a guide to making communication work within the unique rhythms of your relationship. You'll learn why miscommunication happens and how to prevent it.

Inside, we'll explore practical ways to move past defensiveness, navigate hard conversations, and repair disconnection before it deepens. You'll also gain a better understanding of how your nervous system, and your partner's, shapes the way you show up. This awareness helps you work with each other's reactions, not against them.

You'll see how small, intentional shifts in the way you speak and listen can lead to meaningful change. And rather than just talk, this book gives you real tools and practical behaviors that help you build connections in ways you may not have thought possible.

What Informs Wholehearted Communication

The tools in this book are grounded in research and informed by well-established models in relational and emotional health. A fuller list of key influences appears on page 247. Below are a few of the core frameworks that shaped this work.

- ▶ **Nonviolent Communication (NVC)** helps you name and share your feelings and needs without blame. It fosters empathy and creates space for real understanding.
- ▶ **Mindfulness** helps you stay present and responsive instead of defaulting to old habits or knee-jerk reactions.
- ▶ **Polyvagal Theory** teaches how your nervous system affects communication and how to shift from protection back to connection.
- ▶ **Dialectical Behavior Therapy (DBT)** strengthens your emotional regulation so you can navigate hard interactions more effectively.

Together, these frameworks helped me shape an approach that's clear, grounded, and, best of all, doable. Because in the end, Wholehearted Communication is more than just talking. It's about how you love.

My work is also informed by training in three leading relationship methodologies: Imago Therapy, the Gottman Method, and Emotionally Focused Therapy (EFT). Each contributes specific insights and tools that are now part of Wholehearted Communication.

- ▶ **Imago Therapy** revealed how early relational wounds shape present-day dynamics. It taught me that conflict is not a failure. It's a doorway to healing, especially when supported by structured, reflective dialogue.
- ▶ **The Gottman Method** provided research-based tools for identifying destructive patterns, understanding the emotional and phys-

iological roots of conflict, and learning which issues can be solved and which need to be consciously managed over time.

▶ **Emotionally Focused Therapy (EFT)** highlighted the essential role of emotional bonds and secure attachment. It helped me look beneath surface behaviors to the deeper needs driving them, and how partners can create emotional safety, even during conflict.

By weaving these insights together, Wholehearted Communication offers a clear and compassionate path toward greater emotional safety and a deeper understanding.

If you've ever felt misunderstood, stuck in the same patterns, or unsure how to say what you really feel, you are not alone. But what if communication could feel easier? What if it helped you feel seen instead of defensive?

In the chapters that follow, you'll discover:

▶ How to disagree without disconnecting
▶ How to express your needs, emotions, and desires without blame or defensiveness
▶ How to move from self-protection to connection
▶ How to stay connected through life's changes
▶ How to use communication as a path to deeper intimacy

No Stigma. No Judgment. Just Effective Tools.

Wholehearted Communication doesn't replace therapy for all couples, but it may for some. It's an invitation to approach communication as a skill you can practice and strengthen, no matter where your relationship stands today.

If you're holding this book, chances are you're craving more connection, more understanding, and a little more peace between you and your partner.

This book is for you if you've ever:

▶ Felt unheard or misunderstood in conversations
▶ Wanted to stop repeating the same argument on loop
▶ Longed for communication to feel easier, clearer, and less draining
▶ Felt the weight of a silence so heavy you didn't know how to break it.

The Power of Small Shifts

These tools work like Legos: they stack. You don't need to overhaul your entire relationship overnight to feel a difference. Change comes in small, consistent shifts. When you pause before reacting, focus on what matters, and listen with curiosity, these shifts are the building blocks of intimate communication. With practice, you'll begin to recognize what works, what doesn't, and how to reset without spiraling.

You'll catch yourself before snapping. You'll sit in the discomfort instead of deflecting. You'll make one better choice, then another. Slowly, your conversations will start to reflect the love you feel.

Wholehearted Communication is never about being right or winning. In a relationship, either you both win or you both lose. The goal is always connection, especially when things are hard. Each small shift creates momentum for the next.

Wiggle Room

This is a simple example of how small, intentional shifts can stop an interaction from going sideways.

After a long day, Jordan came home exhausted. When Riley asked what was wrong, Jordan snapped, "Nothing. I don't want to talk about it."

At this point, things could have easily gone sideways fast. Riley could have taken it personally. Could have assumed Jordan was mad. Could have shut down. Or fired back something like, 'Well, excuse me for caring.'

Instead, Riley paused and took a breath.

"I get that you don't want to talk right now," Riley said. "Just know I'm here when you're ready."

That one choice changed the trajectory of the night.

Riley gave Jordan wiggle room. Space to be human. Space to have an irritable reaction without personalizing it. Room to reset without it becoming a bad night. The goal isn't perfection. It's grace, curiosity, and the willingness to let each other be human.

Later that evening, Jordan sat down beside Riley. "I didn't mean to snap earlier. I'm sorry. Today was just a lot."

Riley nodded and squeezed Jordan's hand. "I wondered if you might have had a rough day. Thanks for circling back and letting me in on how you are."

Wiggle room doesn't mean pretending nothing happened. If the behavior continues without change or repair, a conversation still needs to happen. It just happens once both people are regulated.

If you can relate to Riley and Jordan, that's not surprising. Throughout this book, you'll encounter examples of couples and conversations that reflect common patterns I've seen over nearly three decades of working with couples. Our struggles are often more shared than we realize. These examples are drawn from themes that show up again and again in therapy sessions, retreats, workshops, and yes, sometimes from the living room couch in my own home. Names and identifying details have been changed, and some examples are composites, created to protect privacy while capturing what these moments often feel like.

Connection isn't about never messing up. It's about trusting that when things get messy, repair is possible. That you can return to each other. That begins with curiosity instead of self-protection.

And, to be clear, couples who practice this don't eliminate conflict. That's not even the goal. The right kind of conflict is healthy. Instead, they shorten the distance between rupture and repair. They feel more understood. More emotionally safe. More connected.

Because communication is how we find our way back when we lose our footing with the person we love.

Why Your Brain Makes Communication Harder Than It Needs to Be

Your brain is wired to keep you safe, not to help you have emotionally honest conversations. When something feels off in your relationship, your nervous system doesn't stop to analyze. It just reacts.

Maybe you raise your voice or interrupt. Maybe you shut down or walk away. Maybe you rush to fix it so you don't have to feel so much. These are not conscious choices. They are automatic responses to perceived danger.

And here's the kicker: it doesn't even matter if the threat is real. Your body reacts anyway. You were built for speed, not precision.

Most of us default to one (or more) of four survival strategies:

- ▶ **Fight:** You get louder, interrupt, or become defensive.
- ▶ **Flight:** You avoid the conversation or check out.
- ▶ **Freeze:** You feel stuck or can't find the right words.
- ▶ **Fix:** You move quickly to smooth things over or solve the problem, skipping the emotional layer.

Many couples feel relieved when they learn this. What once felt like a personal failure starts to make sense as an automatic nervous system response. And automatic responses can be worked with.

Some people also experience additional survival responses, such as fawning (appeasing to stay safe) or flopping (shutting down altogether). These tend to appear when the nervous system becomes overwhelmed beyond fight, flight, freeze, or fix. When this happens, it may look like going numb, feeling foggy, dissociating, or withdrawing completely. We'll talk more about this later, but if this feels familiar, know that your nervous system learned this as a last-resort way to survive.

You may think your partner is being difficult or trying to push your buttons on purpose. But what is usually happening is much simpler. It is two nervous systems under stress, each doing its best to stay safe. Both are self-protecting instead of connecting.

The good news is that this can change. With practice, you will learn how to communicate more effectively and use your words to build trust, intimacy, and a relationship that feels stable and connected.

One more thing before we dig in.

It's completely normal if some of this feels confusing at first. You're being introduced to new ways of understanding yourself, your partner, and how conversations unfold under stress. That takes time to settle.

There is no right order and no wrong pace. However you choose to move through this material will be the right way for you.

"We are born in relationship, we are wounded in relationship, and we can be healed in relationship."

- HARVILLE HENDRIX

CHAPTER 2

The Purpose of Relationships

Growth and Self-Discovery

Relationships Are Your Greatest Investment

Committing to sharing your life with another is one of the most significant investments you will ever make. Think about it: when you commit to sharing your life with someone, you are deciding that out of all the people in the world, your life will be better if you share it with them.

That is a pretty big deal, considering there are some eight billion humans in the world.

Relationships are like an empty bucket: they are nothing until you put something in them. And what they become is determined by what, exactly, you add. Because of this, you can only expect to get out of your relationship (bucket) what at least one of you puts into it. So, if you want kindness, you must put kindness into it. If you want adventure, you must put adventure into it.

The same is true if you put in negativity, insensitivity, or indifference. You get what you give, for better or worse. This is why I consider relationships our greatest investment. At their best, a relationship combines the best of each partner so that both are better in the end. When you contribute your unique strengths to the relationship, you each benefit and your life experience expands.

When you view your relationship as an investment and recognize that everything you give to your relationship is something you, too, will benefit from, it makes it easier to give more freely. The more you give, the more you get.

Your relationship is also one of your greatest teachers. Notice I didn't say that your partner is your best teacher. The lessons come from your relationship, the dance of interaction that can activate old wounds and hidden hurts. Healing occurs when your partner shows up in ways that are loving, kind, and understanding.

According to the Imago Theory, we are drawn to partners with an uncanny ability to recreate the feelings we experienced with our primary caregivers and important others (siblings, grandparents, and other significant people on whom we depended throughout our childhood).

That is why, when people say, "You feel like home to me," it indicates that you have successfully attracted someone who can help you recreate some of the feelings you experienced growing up. That sense of, "Yep, I know this feeling; I've been here before."

Now, this is where things get interesting. Because our partners have such a knack for provoking such familiar feelings in us, as our attachment to our partner grows, so does our unconscious association, linking them to all of the important others that came before. This can be both good and bad. When their behaviors resonate with the most positive experiences we've had in the past, we feel full of love. When their behaviors and ways of interacting with us resonate with past experiences that were negative, we feel the same unhealed wounds and hurts we felt when we were younger.

The Imago theory says we are built to heal, and when we are wounded *in* relationships, we naturally seek healing *through* our relationships. That's why you can spend time alone after a breakup, "working on yourself," focusing on healing.

But then comes the twist.

When you step back into a relationship, you realize the work you did while you were single isn't translating into new behaviors. Turns out, many of the "muscles" we exercise in a relationship cannot be practiced alone. While there is value in reflecting on past relationship choices, including what worked and what didn't, and how you could have shown up differently, the reality is that we can't apply these insights until we are in a relationship again.

Frustrating, right?

That's because we need people to help us heal the hurts that came from people. It's relational work. While solo healing can make us stronger and more self-aware, healing within a relationship requires a partner who is willing to do the work too. Not just any partner, but one who wants to grow alongside you.

And if you happen to be with a partner who does not want to read this book, get help, or maybe does not even see a problem, keep doing this work for yourself. When you commit to your own growth, whether your partner joins you or not, things begin to change. Even if you grow and they do not, your relationship will shift. When one person in a dance changes their steps, the other has no choice but to adjust.

Our Dance of Interaction

What does all of this have to do with communication?

Everything.

The greater resonance you have with how it feels to interact with your partner, and how it felt to be in a relationship with important others (parents, siblings, and other important influences on your development), the more likely you are to recreate a similar dance of interaction.

That doesn't mean your partner is acting like your mom or dad. And it doesn't mean they're doing anything wrong.

It just means your nervous system recognizes patterns. If something about the way your partner responds to you feels like something you've felt before, your body reacts. Even if the situation is completely different, the emotional response feels the same.

When your partner pulls away, you might feel abandoned the way you did as a child. When they criticize you, it might bring back the same feeling you had when nothing you did was ever good enough. That response happens quickly, and it often feels bigger than whatever is happening right now.

This does not mean you are overreacting. You're responding to something real. It's just that the pain is not new, and whatever is being stirred up now is being multiplied by the pain of the past. Your pain didn't start with your partner. It started before you met. That's the power of this work. When you begin to notice these patterns, you can become conscious of the dance and intentionally change the steps so that you can feel the way you want.

And how do these old wounds get healed?

Change begins with self-awareness. But the catch is, you can't force awareness. It has to be reflected back to you, usually in the most inconvenient, uncomfortable ways. And that is the real power of partnership. When we fall in love, we hand someone a front-row ticket to our lives. It is one of the most vulnerable things we'll ever do. We give them access to our best moments and, inevitably, the parts of us we'd rather keep offstage.

As we grow together, our partner's words, tone, and actions bump up against old stories and unhealed hurts. It's rarely intentional, and it's always revealing. The way each of us reacts to those activations becomes our "dance of interaction," a pattern shaped by the protective habits we learned long before this relationship began.

When you start noticing your moves, especially the ones that show up when you are hurt, you can use that pain to become more aware of the wounds that are seeking healing through your relationship. Every interaction, even the difficult ones, becomes a roadmap for healing.

This kind of growth takes honest communication and a genuine willingness to do the work. Wholehearted Communication is here to guide you through that process and help you do it with as much clarity, compassion, and effectiveness as possible.

Relationships as Catalysts for Growth

Real growth doesn't happen in your comfort zone. Relationships will pull you out of that space more than just about anything else. Sometimes gently, sometimes not. That's part of the deal.

Being in a relationship means facing parts of yourself you might have worked hard to avoid. This includes everything you've pushed down, denied, or never had the chance to fully understand. And often, it's your partner who brings all of this to the surface. Not because they're doing anything wrong, but because something in their behavior or tone activates something in you that hasn't been fully healed.

You might not even realize what's happening. One minute things are fine, and the next, you're in a full-blown reaction. Maybe they asked for space and your chest tightened with panic. Or maybe they made a comment that left you feeling invisible, and before you know it, you're defensive, shutting down, or trying harder to be seen.

When something gets stirred up and you feel off-center, those reactions are invitations. Invitations to get curious, to pay attention, and to ask yourself, "What just got activated in me? What do I need right now that I didn't get back then?"

Much of how you show up in relationships is based on programming. What you learned from your family. What the culture taught you about your worth. What past relationships showed you about love and safety. These patterns can appear as though they are part of your personality, like this is just who you are. But patterns not set in stone.

You can change how you show up, but it requires intention. Conscious communication means paying attention to your body, your thoughts, and your urges. It means noticing the familiar loop and choosing to respond differently.

This is where self-awareness becomes your greatest tool. When you can notice your triggers without letting them run the show, you open the door to something new. And every time you do that, even a little, you grow.

How Communication Impacts Relationship Satisfaction

Dr. John Gottman's research shows that functional couples maintain a 5-to-1 ratio of positive to negative interactions. Happier couples have a ratio closer to 20-to-1. This doesn't mean you should avoid hard conversations or pretend everything is fine. It simply means that kindness, curiosity, and generosity need to show up more often than criticism, defensiveness, or contempt.

Every negative interaction is expensive. It costs you nineteen positive interactions just to break even. That's the emotional economy of lasting relationships.

Let's say your partner forgets to grab the milk again. You could roll your eyes and mutter, "Of course you forgot." Or you could say, "I know you've got a lot on your mind. Can you grab it tomorrow?" One response creates tension. The other keeps the connection intact. These moments seem small, but they matter. Over time, they add up and either strengthen the relationship or slowly wear it down.

Even in strong relationships, missteps and misunderstandings happen. That's part of being human. What makes the difference is how you handle those missteps.

Conflict is Inevitable

Conflict is a part of every relationship. In fact, couples who avoid conflict entirely are often less healthy than those who know how to engage with it directly. You and your partner don't need to agree on everything. In fact, you won't. You don't have to see the world the same way. What is important is how you show up when you disagree.

When conflict surfaces, your response says more about whether you feel emotionally safe in that moment than about the issue itself. There are clear signs that conflict has gone off track. Dr. John Gottman calls them the Four Horsemen: criticism, contempt, defensiveness, and stonewalling.

Each of the Four Horsemen is a sign that connection is breaking down:

1. **Criticism** points the finger and makes your partner the problem.
2. **Defensiveness** blocks empathy and shifts the blame.
3. **Stonewalling** shuts the conversation down completely.
4. **Contempt** communicated through eye rolls, sarcasm, or mocking cuts the deepest. It doesn't just say "I'm upset." It says "You're beneath me." Of all of these, contempt is the most dangerous. It erodes connection faster than almost anything else.

These aren't signs that your relationship is broken. They're signals. And once you learn to recognize them, you can interrupt the automatic response and choose a new path. You can reset. You can begin again.

Moving into Self-Awareness

Understanding relationships as mirrors and catalysts for growth is the first step toward mastering Wholehearted Communication. When you see your relationship not as a problem to solve but as an opportunity to grow, you create the foundation for the open, curious, and compassionate communication that Wholehearted Communication offers.

Relationships invite you to see yourself more clearly, grow beyond your self-protective programming, and build a deeper connection with the person you love. But recognizing these patterns is just the first step. The real transformation happens in how you communicate with yourself and your partner. How do you break old patterns? How do you express your needs without falling into the same conflicts?

That's where Wholehearted Communication begins. It is more than just an exchange of words. It is about how those words and the emotions beneath them make your partner feel. When we bring intention to how we speak and listen, communication becomes a path to deeper connection. When we do not, it becomes a wedge.

Your first step is self-awareness. Noticing your automatic reactions. Understanding where they come from. That is where we will go next.

II.

UNDERSTANDING YOURSELF

"Awareness is
the greatest agent
for change."

- ECKHART TOLLE

CHAPTER 3

Self-Awareness in Relationships

In relationships, there's no such thing as "not communicating." Every sigh, glance, or choice to remain silent sends a message. We are constantly communicating. Because of this, developing a greater sense of self-awareness is critical. It allows us to communicate consciously and intentionally so that the messages we intend to send are the messages received.

How often do the messages you send get misinterpreted? Most intimate communication is filtered through tone, body language, and assumptions, leading to unintended misunderstandings. Without self-awareness, you may unintentionally send messages that cause tension or push your partner away.

How "Just Being Myself" May Not Always Work

A common relationship myth is that you should be accepted just as you are. While accepting one another is important, that does not eliminate the need to examine and improve your interactions. This is called personal growth, and for any relationship to remain stable and satisfying, you and your partner must continually examine and address whether or not your participation in your relationship is helping or hurting.

"I was this way when you met me" is often a way of pushing back against growth. It tends to appear when change feels risky. In my work, it's rarely about unwillingness and more often about fear.

When you partner, you transition from "me" to "we," and everything you do or say has the potential to impact the other. To dismiss feedback about the impact of your behavior on your partner is to stall personal and relational growth.

The Business of Love

Relationships are like a business. You and your partner are co-investors in the business of love. If your relationship isn't producing the outcomes you want, things like affection, playfulness, kindness, support, ease, or emotional safety, then it's time to look at what's preventing your success. Just like any business that wants to grow, you have to pay attention to what's not working and be willing to change it.

That means letting go of habits that drain the relationship and replacing them with practices that support your shared values and goals. That's just good business. And in this case, the return on your investment is a more connected, more fulfilling relationship.

Self-awareness is how we do this. It is the practice of tuning into your inner world, thoughts, feelings, and reactions, and understanding how they influence your interactions with others.

To build this self-awareness, we will explore your inner world through two key lenses: the "Language of the Mind" and the "Language of the Body." Then, we will look at how to use that awareness to change your actions.

Here is the path we will take:

> ▶ **The Language of the Mind:** This is your internal narrative, the cognitive part of your experience. We will explore the crucial difference between Facts (the objective truths) and Stories (the narratives we create about them).
> ▶ **The Language of the Body:** This is your internal emotional and physical experience. We will explore:
>> • **The Signals:** Your Emotions, Feelings, and Sensations (the "input" your body gives you).

- **The Drivers:** Your core Needs and the automatic Urges they create (the "output" they demand).

▶ **The Path to Connection:** Once we understand our inner world, we will explore what we do with that awareness. We will look at our automatic, protective reactions (Self-Protection) and how to replace them with conscious, intentional choices (Effective Actions).

Self-awareness is at the heart of Wholehearted Communication. Understanding the interplay between your mind's stories, your body's signals, and your automatic reactions is the foundation for change. These elements shape how you interact with your partner; the more aware you are of them, the clearer and more intentional your communication becomes.

In the following chapters, you'll find:

▶ A deeper discussion of each concept.

▶ Practical tools to develop self-awareness in that area.

▶ Real-life examples of how mastering these skills can transform communication and strengthen relationships.

A Note on Pace

We've covered a lot so far. This material is not designed for speed reading. When you're ready, we'll unpack the difference between facts and stories, why that distinction matters, and how separating the two can reduce misunderstandings, improve communication, and support connection in your relationship.

"We don't see things as they are; we see them as we are."

CHAPTER 4

Facts and Stories

The Language of the Mind

The "Language of the Mind" is the constant, internal narrative you tell yourself about your world. It's the voice that interprets events and assigns them meaning. This language is powerful, but it can also be wildly ineffective, especially in a relationship. That's because it often blurs the line between two very different things: the *facts* of what happened and the *stories* we tell ourselves about them.

We've all been there. What starts as "Hey, can you take out the trash?" somehow turns into a conversation about *everything* that's ever gone wrong in your relationship. It's never just about the trash, is it?

You ask your partner if they'd like to grab dinner, but they don't immediately respond. Suddenly, your mind jumps to conclusions: *They're mad at me. They're ignoring me. They don't care about spending time with me.* Meanwhile, your partner is distracted and focused on a work email they're trying to finish before it's too late. Because you've attached a story to their silence, you react from that place; you snap at them or withdraw, believing they're upset.

Every day, I hear couples clinging to their stories, convinced they are facts. The higher the emotional charge, the tighter that grip becomes. Once things slow down and there is room to sort facts from feelings, most can see the difference. They often say, "It was the only thing that made sense to me."

Your partner, just trying to focus on their work, feels confused and hurt by your reaction. What should have been a simple conversation about dinner turns into an emotional conflict, all over something that wasn't accurate in the first place.

This is what happens when we confuse facts with stories.

What is a Fact and What is a Story?

A fact is neutral, observable, hearable, measurable, and verifiable. It's what actually happened. A story is your interpretation of that fact. It's what we tell ourselves about what happened. And because stories are shaped by your past experiences, fears, or insecurities, they are not always true.

For example:

- ▶ **Fact:** Your partner left the dishes in the sink.
- ▶ **Story**: They don't appreciate everything I do around here.
- ▶ **Fact:** Partner signed up for a late shift.
- ▶ **Story:** They'd rather be at work than with me.

When we don't separate facts from stories, we react to the story, not the actual event. And that's how small interactions turn into unnecessary arguments.

How Your Brain Turns Experience Into Story

Your brain is constantly working behind the scenes to create order and meaning out of everything you experience. When your nervous system takes in raw information such as what you see, hear, smell, taste, touch, or sense emotionally, it sends that data to your brain. Your brain then sorts through it, compares it to your past experiences, and organizes it into a story.

Stories are the way our brain is programmed to make quick sense of the world and our safety in it. This is how humans are built to survive. The brain is always predicting and interpreting, using patterns from the past to navigate the present.

Trauma experts like Dr. Bessel van der Kolk have shown that our bodies store these emotional imprints. When something triggers a familiar feeling, like fear, sadness, or rejection, we react as if the past is happening all over again. And it happens so fast that we often don't stop to question whether the story we're telling ourselves is true.

Think of it like outdated spyware on a computer. It is still scanning for old threats that are no longer dangerous and may even miss the new ones that are. Your nervous system is doing its job, but sometimes it gets it wrong.

When Jordan was growing up, her mother would go quiet and give her a look when something was wrong. Nothing was said, but the message was clear. Jordan learned early what that silence meant.

Years later, when Riley goes silent or makes a similar face, Jordan's body reacts before her mind does. She feels tense and shut out, even when Riley isn't upset at all.

Jordan isn't reacting to Riley alone. Jordan's nervous system is responding to what's happening now and to an old emotional memory that just got activated.

This is where stories come in.

Consider the difference between a fact and the story we tell about it.

- ▸ **Fact:** "I woke up at 5 a.m. today, and you woke up at 8 a.m." This is an objective, verifiable truth. It's just data.
- ▸ **Story / Interpretation:** "I woke up *so much earlier* than you." This statement adds a layer of judgment and comparison. The

words "so much earlier" are a personal interpretation. They might imply, "I'm more productive," or "I'm resentful that I have to wait so long before you get up."

▸ **Story / Belief:** "I just don't need as much sleep as you do." This is an even bigger story. It's a generalized belief or a statement of identity, not a measurable fact for a specific day.

These stories, the interpretations and beliefs, are what influence how you think, how you speak, and how you respond in relationships. Distinguishing between a fact (the raw data) and the story (the interpretation) is an essential skill in Wholehearted Communication.

Examples of Facts vs. Stories

Let's look at some typical relationship scenarios where our stories can lead us astray. These examples show how everyday misunderstandings stem from our stories.

The Forgotten Text

Fact: My partner didn't respond to my text for four hours.
Story: They must be avoiding me because they're upset about something I did.

It's easy to assume silence means disinterest or avoidance, especially when feeling vulnerable. But there are plenty of other reasons for a delayed response. Maybe they got caught up at work, misplaced their phone, their phone battery died, or they simply needed a break from screens. Instead of assuming the worst, pause and consider alternative explanations before reacting.

The Interrupted Conversation

Fact: My partner interrupted me.
Story: They don't respect me or what I have to say.

When someone cuts us off mid-sentence, it can feel dismissive. But not all interruptions signal disrespect. They could stem from excitement, a misunderstanding, or even an attempt to relate. Before assuming your partner doesn't care about your thoughts, try saying, "I'd love to finish sharing my point before you jump in. Can I keep going?"

The Quiet Car Ride

Fact: My partner was silent during the drive home.
Story: They're mad at me because of what I said earlier.

Like the forgotten text, silence can feel unsettling, especially when we're already feeling uncertain. But what if their quietness isn't about you at all? Maybe they're mentally processing something from their day, feeling overwhelmed, or simply enjoying the stillness. Instead of assuming frustration, ask with curiosity: "Hey, you've been quiet. Everything okay?"

Simply noticing when a story might be present is already a meaningful shift. Even pausing to wonder, *"Is this a fact, or is this a story I'm telling myself?"* is progress. This work is subtle, and it can be surprisingly difficult, especially when emotions are running high.

This work is about awareness. It's about noticing what's happening and bringing more attention to the present. Perfection isn't required, and there's no rigid standard to meet.

This is also not an invitation to police each other's language or correct your partner in the middle of a conversation. No one feels safer or more connected when they're being fact-checked or told they're "in a story." That tends to escalate things, not repair them. If you think your partner is in a story, the move is not correction. The move is curiosity. When you approach this with humility instead of precision, it becomes a tool for connection rather than control.

If you're feeling a little full right now, pause. This is a lot of new mental wiring. We're going to keep making it simpler.

Spot How Stories Take Over

As you can see from these examples, it's not always the facts that cause distress; it's the meaning we assign to them. Small interactions can become big conflicts when we mistake our assumptions for reality. This is why it's important to recognize when stories take over our thinking and learn to separate them from facts.

And once you start noticing your stories, new options open up.

Prevent Miscommunication Early

Let's say your partner comes home, closes the door loudly, and doesn't say a word. At first, you might think the fact is that the door slammed loudly. But here's the thing: "slammed loudly" is a story. It's an interpretation of the volume and action of the door, and it is influenced by your perspective.

A fact would sound like this: "I heard the door close from the bedroom, three rooms away." This describes what happened without adding any subjective judgment or emotional tone. It gives a neutral, clear picture that anyone in the house could agree on.

A story would sound like this: "They slammed the door because they're angry with me." Notice how much is packed into this statement. First, you've described the door closing as "slamming," a charged word. Then, you've attached the assumption that they're angry. Finally, you've made it personal, assuming their supposed anger is directed at you. A lot is packed into the sound of a door closing!

This is where communication can start to jump the tracks. When you respond from your story instead of the facts, you are reacting to your interpretation, not the event itself. Maybe the door closed loudly. Instead of asking what happened, you assume your partner is angry and snap at them.

You're not responding to the sound of the door. You're responding to the story your brain created about it.

Check Your Stories

Responding from the facts sounds like this: "I heard the door close from the bedroom, and it surprised me. Is everything okay?" This way the focus is on your experience without making assumptions about their intentions or emotions. It opens the door (no slamming here) for conversation instead of confrontation.

This simple shift, checking your story, can change everything.

In this example, the fact gives you a neutral starting point: The door closed loudly enough to be heard from the bedroom. The story, they slammed the door because they're angry with me, is worth examining before you bring it into the conversation. Considering other possible explanations will offer perspective and invite a better, more accurate understanding.

What else could explain this? Maybe the wind caught the door, or perhaps they had a rough day and didn't realize how loud it was. Separating the facts from the story gives you space to approach the situation with curiosity rather than judgment.

This one shift can transform your communication. When you focus on facts, you remove the emotional charge that stories often carry. You create space for your partner to respond without defensiveness and leave room for understanding and connection.

Recognize Your Story Filters

When we treat our stories as truth, we trap our partner in an alternate reality that we've made up. The cure for this is a focus on facts. Facts are neutral. They just are.

In situations where you truly need to act fast, like avoiding a car accident or responding to immediate danger, this kind of instinctive meaning-making is helpful. It keeps you safe. But in everyday life, where the threat is emotional rather than physical, your mind can easily go too far. It creates a sense of urgency or danger that typically does not exist.

Your mind is wired to create meaning where there is missing or incomplete information. It is instinctive to fill in the blanks.

Notice Your Story

The good news is, you don't have to stay stuck there. The first step is to notice the story you're telling yourself.

When you feel a strong emotional reaction, pause and ask yourself, *What are the facts?* By bringing your awareness to what actually happened, you create space to challenge the story and rewrite it in a way that fits the present more accurately.

Your brain and body have been doing their best to protect you. And if you're reading this, your nervous system has a 100 percent success rate at keeping you alive. I mean, those are some good stats, right?

Yes, it might overreact, misfire, and create unnecessary struggle from time to time. But it is still doing its job. And that matters.

Give it time and a little intention, and you begin to see how your nervous system works. It has a habit of pulling old experiences into brand-new interactions. Suddenly, you realize you're consulting your four-year-old, ten-year-old, or fifteen-year-old self for guidance. They mean well, but none of them are qualified for the job.

We Hear What We Fear

Our insecurities, doubts, and worries act like filters, sensitizing us to specific cues in our interactions with the people we care about most. But when we recognize these filters, we gain the power to question them and choose a different response.

For example, if rejection is part of your life experience with important others you relied on for survival, your system may be pre-conditioned to notice things that feel like rejection. As a result, you may react to things that feel like distance or dismissal the same way you did growing up.

Let's go back to that unanswered text. The fact is, they haven't responded yet. But the story can vary wildly depending on your emotional state. If you're feeling calm and grounded, you might think, *They must be busy. I'll hear from them later.* If you're feeling vulnerable or anxious, it might turn into, *They're mad at me*, or even, *They don't care enough to reply.*

In one of my classes for *The Art of Wholehearted Communication*, I shared an example about an unanswered text and asked how people would interpret it. About ten participants responded, and there were nine different interpretations. *They're running late. They're mad at me. I'm not a priority. Their phone died. They're ignoring me.*

Only two people shared a similar explanation. Each story revealed far more about the person telling it than about the unanswered text itself.

Do you see how the same fact can lead to entirely different stories? And how those stories, in turn, shape how you feel and act? You might feel hurt, resentful, or defensive if you believe they're ignoring you because they're upset. You might send a follow-up text like, "Why are you ignoring me?" or, "Are you mad?" which could escalate tension. But if you believe they're just busy, you're more likely to wait it out or send a lighthearted message like, "Hope your day's going okay!"

I once worked with a couple who we'll call Alex and Sam. When they had strong disagreements, Alex withdrew, sometimes retreating to the bedroom or taking a walk without letting Sam in on what was happening. This left Sam feeling abandoned. And every time, Sam's inner narrative was the same: *Alex doesn't care enough to stay and work this out with me.*

But what was really happening? Alex wasn't leaving out of indifference. Alex was overwhelmed by the intensity of the interaction and how it felt in Alex's body. Alex stepped away to create space to regulate emotions and return with a clearer head.

For Sam, though, this was about more than just their relationship with Alex. It tapped into an older, familiar feeling of not being chosen, of having to compete for attention, and of wondering whether his needs mattered enough to be prioritized.

When Sam's parents divorced, Sam's father stopped coming to visit, leaving Sam with the belief that *people I love won't stick around.* So, every time Alex walked out of a difficult conversation, that old story resurfaced, reinforcing the same painful cycle. Without understanding these deeper layers, Alex and Sam kept playing out the past instead of seeing each other clearly in the present.

When we start treating our stories as truth, as Sam did, we are no longer reacting to what's happening but to what we fear *might* be happening. And that's where disconnection begins.

But we can commit to something new and more effective when we recognize that our actions aren't working. The goal is to catch ourselves when we're spinning a story and shift back to the facts.

For example, if your partner is scrolling on their phone while you're talking, it's easy to jump to the story: They don't care. Instead of running with the story, it can help to pause and ask yourself three simple questions:

- ▶ **What are the facts?** While we talked, my partner was on their phone
- ▶ **What are my feelings?** Hurt, unimportant, boring
- ▶ **What is the story?** I am not interesting enough to hold my partner's attention.

When you notice a story taking shape, it helps to slow down and consider a few other possibilities that are also grounded in fact.

Alternative Story 1: My partner is playing a mindless game to decompress while listening. They might not even realize that it comes across as disinterest.

Alternative Story 2: My partner was in the middle of finishing something important when I started talking. I might have interrupted without realizing it, and they're just trying to wrap it up before fully engaging with me.

Alternative Story 3: My partner is unaware of how deeply engaged they are with their phone. It's not that they don't care; they lack awareness of what is happening.

Remember: Facts are neutral; stories are judgment. When a story arises, hold it loosely and leave space for the best possible interpretation. We're wired to create stories. It's how our brains make sense of the world and protect us from uncertainty. While the goal is to stay grounded in facts, stories will still arise. When that happens, hold your stories loosely and leave space for the best possible interpretation.

Quiz: Fact or Story?

For each of the following statements, decide whether it is a fact or a story. If it's a fact, simply mark it as "Fact." If it's a story, mark it as "Story," identify the assumption that makes it a "Story," and correct the sentence so it only includes the fact.

1. My partner left the kitchen without cleaning up because they were lazy.

2. They didn't call me back all day.

3. My partner didn't hold my hand because they were embarrassed to be seen with me.

4. My partner was quiet during dinner because they were upset with me.

5. My partner came home at 9 p.m.

6. My partner forgot to text me because they didn't care about my feelings.

7. My partner didn't ask me about my day because they were too self-centered.

8. They left for work without saying goodbye.

9. My partner didn't respond to my message because they were mad at me.

10. My partner has been on their phone for an hour straight.

Answers

Here are the correct answers and corrections for the sentences that were stories.

1. **Story -** **Correction:** My partner left the kitchen without cleaning up. (The assumption that they are lazy is the story.)

2. **Fact**

3. **Story -** **Correction:** My partner didn't hold my hand. (The assumption that they are embarrassed to be seen with me is the story.)

4. **Story** **Correction:** My partner did not initiate conversation during dinner. (The assumption that they are upset with me is the story.)

5. **Fact**

6. **Story -** **Correction:** My partner didn't text me. (The assumption that it's because they don't care about my feelings is the story.)

7. **Story -** **Correction:** My partner didn't ask me about my day. (The assumption that it's because they are self-centered is the story.)

8. **Fact**

9. **Story -** **Correction**: My partner didn't respond to my message. (The assumption that it's because they are mad at me is the story.)

10. **Fact**

"Our emotions are not to be held and cherished and protected; they are to be felt, experienced, and used to inform our lives.

- BRENÉ BROWN

CHAPTER 5

The Language of the Body

As humans, we all come equipped with an emotional guidance system. Think of it like your built-in GPS. This incredible part of being human generates a constant feedback loop and a personal roadmap, helping you steer your life. The trick is learning how to tune in and understand its signals.

When your choices and experiences align with your values, goals, and what really matters to you, your emotional guidance system responds with positive emotions. It's your inner voice saying, *You're on the right track. Keep going!*

However, when you feel uncomfortable or experience negative emotions, your guidance system is alerting you that you're off track. These emotions aren't random; they're signals guiding you toward a more authentic, satisfying life. The more closely you listen to and trust this inner feedback, the easier it becomes to handle challenges, resolve conflicts, and meet your needs.

If facts and stories are the language of our mind, our feelings and emotions are the language of our body. In Wholehearted Communication, our goal is to become fluent in both.

Every emotional experience begins in the body, with sensations.

This chapter isn't meant to be read quickly. If you notice yourself skimming, that's information. Slow down. Take a breath. Let your body stay with you as you read.

Sensations

Every emotion begins as a sensation. Before your mind names it or your story explains it, your body feels it. Sometimes it's the tightening in your chest or the lump in your throat, or maybe a flutter in your stomach. These are your first clues that something inside you is stirring.

Sensations are your body's way of whispering (and sometimes screaming) what your mind hasn't yet put into words. These sensations are like your nervous system's little warning lights saying, *Hey, something's happening here. Pay attention.*

When your nervous system detects danger, it releases chemicals into your bloodstream. This surge can create a kind of chaos inside your body, often leading to emotional dysregulation and triggering a series of physical sensations.

These sensations vary from person to person. The same chemicals can move through two separate bodies and create entirely unique effects, much like how drugs or alcohol affect people differently. Still, whenever your system perceives a threat to your physical or emotional safety, those chemicals tend to follow a predictable pattern.

By learning how your body responds to these shifts, you can anticipate what's happening, track the pattern, and begin to manage the emotional dysregulation that follows.

Take a moment to notice your body right now. Is there tension anywhere? Warmth? Tightness? Nothing at all? There's nothing to fix. Just notice.

Now that you have a sense of how sensations show up in your body, let's look at emotions and feelings themselves.

IDENTIFY YOUR BODY SENSATIONS

Blank Mind	Hot Face/Neck
Body Aches	Hyperventilating
Breathing Fast	Lump in Throat
Clenched Jaw	Nausea
Cold	Neck Tension
Difficulty Swallowing	Numbness
Dizzy	Pulsing
Dry Mouth	Queasy
Dull	Rapid Heartbeat
Energy Rush	Shaking
Face Tight	Shallow Breathing
Facial Tick	Sweating
Floating	Tense Muscles
Heavy Limbs	Tingly
Headache	Weakness

Emotions Are Like the Weather

Think of emotions and feelings as two things that often travel together but are not the same. Most of us lump them into one big category because they show up at the same time and make a lot of noise. But there is a small difference between them, and once you see it, things start to make more sense.

Here is the simplest way to think about it.

For example, rain is just rain. But one person might think, *This ruins everything*, while another thinks, *Good, the garden needs it*. Same weather. Different stories.

If you don't know the difference, life can feel like walking outside without checking the forecast. One minute everything is fine. The next, you're caught in a sudden downpour.

Emotion shows up fast. It is your body saying, *Something just happened.*

Feeling shows up next. It is your mind saying, "Here is what I think that means."

If you do not separate the two, the story you tell yourself can take over before you even realize it. That is when you get swept up in the gust. You stop reacting to the emotion itself and start reacting to the meaning you made of it.

Emotion is the weather.

Feeling is your interpretation of the weather.

When you mix them together, the interpretation becomes the problem. You end up reacting to the feeling (the meaning you created) instead of the emotion (the thing your body simply noticed).

But when you notice the emotion first, you anchor yourself. You can say, "Ah, there is fear," or "There is anger," before your mind decides, *This is a disaster,* or *They do not care,* or *I am not enough.*

That tiny pause changes the whole experience.

You are still having weather, but now you are not inside the storm. You are watching it roll through. And from that place, you can respond instead of react. You can choose the next step instead of being pulled into it.

That is what it means to get your footing back.

Just notice, over the next few days, when weather shows up in your body and when a story quickly follows.

Let's break it down.

A note before we continue:

If this section brings things up for you, that's not a problem. You can stop, take a break, or come back later. Understanding emotions is a practice, not a race.

Primary Emotions

Primary emotions are like changes in the weather; they happen automatically, and you can't control when they happen. Just as you can't control when a storm rolls in, you don't choose to feel startled when something jumps out at you or sad when you experience a loss.

Fear, joy, sadness, anger, surprise, and disgust are universal emotions found across cultures and hardwired into the human brain. They're your body's first responders, designed to help you survive and successfully move through the world.

They go off automatically without your permission.

- ▸ **Fear says:** There's danger. Be alert, protect yourself.
- ▸ **Joy says:** This is good. Connect, keep going.
- ▸ **Sadness says:** Something valuable is lost. Slow down, grieve, seek comfort.
- ▸ **Anger says:** A boundary has been crossed. Stand up, protect what matters.
- ▸ **Surprise says:** Something unexpected just happened. Pause, gather more information.
- ▸ **Disgust says:** This is harmful or toxic. Move away, reject it.

The Speed and Power of Primary Emotions

Primary emotions rise fast, peak quickly, and fade, all within seconds or minutes. Consider your reaction to a close call while driving your vehicle.

The intensity and duration of your primary emotions depend on several factors.

- ▶ **The trigger**: A minor scare fades fast. A major one lingers longer.
- ▶ **Your history**: If you've been in a car accident, even a close call might send your body into overdrive.
- ▶ **Your ability to process emotions**: Some people can shake things off, while others stay stuck in their feelings longer.

Someone without a trauma history might laugh off a close call. Someone with a history of feeling unsafe in the world might feel shaky for hours. That's how past experiences shape our emotional responses.

Secondary Emotions

Now, let's talk about where things get tangled. Like primary emotions, secondary emotions are still automatic but not universal. Secondary emotions are shaped by your history, values, cultural background, and social environment, and include things like guilt, pride, shame, and jealousy.

Think about it:

- ▶ **Sadness** (primary emotion) might turn into guilt (secondary emotion) if you grew up in a family where expressing sadness was seen as "dramatic" or "selfish."
- ▶ **Fear** (primary emotion) might transform into shame (secondary emotion) if you were raised in an environment that taught you that being afraid makes you weak.
- ▶ **Anger** (primary emotion) might evolve into resentment (secondary emotion) if your life experiences have reinforced the belief that others are responsible for your emotions.

Feelings

Feelings are the way you make sense of what is happening inside you. Two people can face the same situation and have completely different responses, depending on their history, personality, and mindset.

Nervousness before a big presentation might register as excitement for one person and dread for another. The event is the same. The meaning each person makes is different. It is a bit like the difference between the weather and what you choose to wear. You cannot control the weather, but you can choose how to prepare for it.

When you understand this, you can start noticing the moments when your reactions are automatic and the moments when you have room to shift your perspective.

Emotions and Feelings in Action

Imagine you are reading late at night when a loud crash comes from the kitchen. Instantly, your heart pounds, your muscles tense, and your breath speeds up. That is fear, a primary emotion, doing its job.

A moment later, your mind begins sorting through possibilities. Maybe it was the wind. Maybe the cat knocked something over. Maybe it is something more dangerous. This meaning-making is where feelings take shape. They grow out of your beliefs, memories, and assumptions.

What is interesting is that the story you tell yourself about an emotion can completely change your response to it. If you decide it was the cat, you feel relief. If you imagine an intruder, you feel panic. This is the space between emotion and feeling, and this is where your small window of choice lives.

We only feel in the present because emotions arise in response to what is happening right now. Even when a memory or a worry pulls you into the past or future, the emotion still shows up in the present moment.

The Difference Between Feelings and Stories

Knowing the difference between expressing our feelings and making judgments or telling stories about them is crucial in communication. Many people unknowingly use phrases that sound like feelings but are interpretations or assumptions. Here are four common examples:

▶ **I feel LIKE...**

When we say, "I feel like you're mad at me," that's not a feeling. It is an assessment of somebody else. Inserting "feel" before sharing our judgment or opinion doesn't make it a feeling. It might seem more palatable, even kinder. However, it's still not a feeling.

▶ **I feel THAT...**

Whatever follows this is a story. "I feel that you are angry with me." (This is an interpretation, not a feeling.)

▶ **I feel AS IF...**

Whatever follows this is a story. "I feel as if I did something to upset you." (This is an interpretation, not a feeling.)

▶ **I feel YOU...**

Whatever follows this is a story. "I feel you want me to go but aren't telling me." (This is an interpretation, not a feeling.)

Most of us were never taught how to notice and name feelings. Awareness comes first. Change comes later.

There are also adjectives that are often mistaken for emotions but are really interpretations or judgments. These words typically assign blame or suggest that someone else is responsible for how we feel.

As a general rule, words that end in *-ed* tend to place blame. They usually imply that someone else did something to you. For example, if you say you feel *attacked*, it suggests someone attacked you.

Clear, effective communication focuses on facts and feelings. When you do need to express an interpretation or story, the key is to own it. Try saying: **"The story I make up is..."**

Judgment vs. Feeling

A good way to know whether a word is a feeling word is to test it with this formula:

You _____ me.

If the word inserted here makes sense, it is likely a judgment, not a feeling:

- ✗ You rejected me.
- ✗ You attacked me.
- ✗ You criticized me.
- ✗ You abandoned me.
- ✗ You disrespected me.

Because the following sentences do not make sense, they are likely feeling words:

- ✔ You unlovable me.
- ✔ You unimportant me.
- ✔ You alone me.
- ✔ You lonely me.

To say "I feel abandoned" is not the same as naming a feeling. Abandoned is a conclusion about someone else's actions. A better question to ask yourself is: "How does it feel to believe I've been abandoned?" Your genuine emotional experience might be sadness, loneliness, fear, or unworthiness.

To uncover the real emotion underneath a judgment, ask yourself:

"How do I feel when I believe this story?"

This helps shift your attention inward, where you will find your feelings.

The following list gives examples of a story word → followed by feeling words that may indicate your internal experience.

- **Abandoned** → lonely, unsure, powerless, unworthy, afraid
- **Abused** → afraid, hurt, powerless, ashamed
- **Betrayed** → hurt, angry, disoriented, lonely
- **Bullied** → afraid, powerless, overwhelmed, panicked
- **Cheated** → angry, disappointed, hurt, ashamed
- **Criticized** → hurt, embarrassed, insecure, defensive
- **Disrespected** → hurt, angry, frustrated, indignant, small
- **Ignored** → invisible, sad, powerless
- **Insulted** → defensive, shocked, bitter, resentful
- **Invalidated** → angry, hopeless, hurt, discouraged
- **Manipulated** → confused, doubtful, uneasy, resentful
- **Put Down** → angry, hurt, insecure, embarrassed
- **Rejected** → vulnerable, sad, embarrassed
- **Threatened** → scared, anxious, panicked, vulnerable
- **Victimized** → helpless, sad, ashamed, angry
- **Violated** → shocked, ashamed, exposed, numb
- **Wronged** → angry, resentful, hurt, indignant

My Feelings Don't Involve "You"

This next section is about increasing the chances of being understood.

One of the most powerful changes you can make to your emotional communication is to eliminate the word **"you"** when you're talking about your feelings.

Why? Because as soon as the word **"you"** enters the sentence, the focus shifts away from your inner experience and toward the other person's behavior. Instead of revealing how you feel, you're now telling someone what they did or didn't do. And that almost always puts the other person on the defensive.

For example, saying, "I feel like you don't care," is not a feeling. It's an accusation wrapped in emotion. What you're likely feeling underneath that is hurt, sadness, or loneliness. But when you say, "you don't care," your partner is far more likely to defend or argue than to empathize.

Removing the word **"you"** from your vocabulary when naming feelings helps keep the focus where it belongs, on you. Your emotions are valid and worth sharing, but they land more gently and are much more likely to be heard when you speak from your own experience.

Instead of:

"I feel like you don't listen."

Try:
"I feel unheard."
"I feel disconnected."
"I feel sad when I share my feelings and don't get a response."

This doesn't mean you can never talk about your partner's behavior. It means it will go a lot better if you can identify and share your feelings and then, if needed, describe the facts and take responsibility for how you are interpreting them.

That simple shift of dropping **"you"** from emotional language can create more connection, less defensiveness, and a much higher chance of being understood.

Feelings come from within, shaped by how you interpret what is happening around you. They are not about what someone else did or did not do. While another person's actions may influence how you feel, your emotions are still about you. They reflect your values, needs, past experiences, and interpretations, not someone else's.

Naming Your Feelings

Feelings are one-word descriptions of the emotional experience inside your body.

- ▶ I feel sad.
- ▶ I feel mad.
- ▶ I feel glad.
- ▶ I feel afraid.
- ▶ I feel happy.

If you are using an entire sentence or more to describe how you feel, you are not expressing feelings.

It Is a Practice

You cannot have an intimate connection using only your brain. Intimacy is not a brain thing. It is a body thing. Intimacy is not a thought; it is an experience that must be felt. You must access your emotions to have a connected, intimate conversation coming from the heart.

Understanding your emotions can sometimes feel like untangling a knot, messy and overwhelming. **The Feeling Charts** on the following pages simplify this process by organizing emotions into eight core categories:

- ▶ **Anger** (frustration, resentment, irritation)
- ▶ **Sadness** (loneliness, disappointment, grief)
- ▶ **Worry** (anxiety, nervousness, overthinking)
- ▶ **Inadequacy** (self-doubt, insecurity, comparison)

▶ **Alarm** (panic, fear, distress)

▶ **Joy** (happiness, excitement, contentment)

▶ **Inspiration** (motivation, creativity, personal growth)

▶ **Gratitude** (appreciation, connection, fulfillment)

Below, you will find two Feeling Charts: "Needs Unmet" and "Needs Met."

Think of these as your emotional vocabulary expanders. It's easy to know you feel "good" or "bad," but it's much more difficult to identify the kind of "good," or the kind of "bad," you feel. Perhaps you feel "content" versus "elated," or "resentful" versus "lonely." Naming the specific feeling is the first step to understanding it.

▶ The **Needs Unmet** chart lists the painful, uncomfortable emotions. These are your body's most important warning signs, telling you that a core need is not being met and requires your attention.

▶ The **Needs Met** chart lists the positive, comfortable emotions you feel when your core needs are being fulfilled. These are the signals that tell you, "Yes, this is working. You are on the right track."

Use these charts to pinpoint the *specific* feeling you are experiencing. Once you have the word for your feeling, you are ready for the next step: discovering the *need* driving it.

Practice Identifying Feelings

▶ Use the Feeling Chart to check in, identify, and differentiate between your emotions during a challenging moment or at the end of the day.

▶ Start by identifying your core emotions (anger, sadness, joy, etc.).

▶ Reflect on how that emotion manifests in your body. Do you feel tension, heat, or lightness?

▶ Choose one of the core emotions from the chart and notice the specific nuance of that emotion (e.g., is it frustration, resentment, or rage under the category of anger?).

▶ Use the chart as a guide to clarify your feelings and share them with your partner.

To improve self-awareness, distinguish between primary (automatic) and secondary emotions (judgment-based). For example:

▶ A recent emotional event where I felt a strong reaction was

_____.

▶ The **primary emotion** I felt was (anger, fear, sadness).

_____.

▶ **The secondary emotion** (my judgment of my initial emotion) was _____.

If you felt anger (primary emotion) because your partner didn't respond to a message, a secondary emotion might be anger at yourself for being hurt, resentment for feeling neglected, or even self-blame for thinking you should be stronger or not let it affect you. These secondary emotions are more about interpreting the hurt than just acknowledging it.

You don't have to do all of this at once.

If you take one thing from this chapter, let it be this: noticing is already progress. Close the book when you need to. Your nervous system will thank you.

NEEDS UNMET

ANGER
Feeling wronged or violated

Increased heart rate
Heat or flushing
Muscle tension
Restlessness
Chest tightness
Shallow breathing

Annoyed	Exasperated	Irate
Appalled	Frustrated	Irritated
Bitter	Furious	Livid
Contempt	Hostile	Mad
Disdain	Impatient	Outraged
Displeased	Incensed	Repulsed
Enraged	Infuriated	Resentful

WORRY
Uncertainty about something

Chest tightness
Stomach knots
Trembling or shakiness
Sweaty palms
Rapid breathing
Lightheadedness

Anxious	Nervous	Stressed
Edgy	Out-of-control	Suspicious
Fearful	Panicked	Terrified
Fragile	Resistant	Troubled
Frazzled	Restless	Uneasy
Guarded	Scared	Worried
Insecure	Sensitive	

INADEQUACY
Self-blame

Sinking feel in chest/stomach
Slumped posture
Warmth or flushing
Tight throat
Nausea
Urge to withdraw

Ashamed	Inferior	Shameful
Deflated	Insignificant	Small
Embarrassed	Jealous	Unacceptable
Envious	Lost	Undeserving
Guilty	Powerless	Unimportant
Helpless	Remorseful	
Inadequate	Self-conscious	

ALARM
Unexpected negative experience

Startle jolt
Wide eyes or sharp inhale
Goosebumps
Racing heart
Body tension
Shaky or unsteady feeling

Apprehensive	Disgusted	Nauseated
Astonished	Disillusioned	Panicked
Blindsided	Disturbed	Perplexed
Cautious	Doubtful	Shaken
Concerned	Frightened	Shocked
Confused	Hesitant	Startled
Demoralized	Horrified	Tense

SADNESS
Sense of loss or longing

Chest heaviness
Deep sighs
Tight throat
Low energy
Slumped muscles
Hollow or empty feeling

Crushed	Disappointed	Heartbroken
Defeated	Disconnected	Helpless
Dejected	Discouraged	Hopeless
Depressed	Disheartened	Hurt
Desperate	Distant	Isolated
Despondent	Empty	Lonely
Devastated	Grief	Miserable

NEEDS MET

JOYFUL	Positive, pleasurable, uplifting experiences		
Warmth in the chest Lightness in the body Pleasant tingles Increased energy Soft relaxation A sense of openness	Blissful Cheerful Delighted Ecstatic Elated Enthusiastic	Excited Exhilarated Gleeful Happy Jovial Jubilant	Joyful Radiant Rejoicing Thrilled

GRATEFUL	Appreciation of goodness, kindness, or meaningful experience		
Warmth in the chest Full-body softening Ease or calm settling Open, easy breath Grounded	Appreciative Contented Delighted Gracious Harmonious Humble	Lucky Overjoyed Pleased Relaxed Relieved Satisfied	Serene Thankful Touched Warmhearted

INSPIRED	Feeling motivated, uplifted, or stirred to action		
Goosebumps or tingles Upward-moving energy Heightened alertness A rising internal lift Increased vitality	Blissful Cheerful Delighted Ecstatic Elated Enthusiastic	Excited Exhilarated Gleeful Happy Jovial Jubilant	Joyful Radiant Rejoicing Thrilled

Decision-Making Guide

Emotions act as internal guides, helping us make choices by signaling what feels good or bad. Emotions create a feedback loop, letting us know whether we're on track or off track at any given moment. When our needs are met, we feel good, and our emotions send the message: *You're safe. Things are okay.* These positive feelings signal alignment with what matters to us.

Our system raises a flag when we experience negative emotions, urging us to slow down, pay attention, or pivot entirely. Sometimes, these emotions are subtle, like a quiet discomfort, nudging us to reconsider. Other times, they're loud and unmistakable, demanding immediate action.

Understanding your needs is the first step. The next step is understanding what happens when those needs *aren't* met. That *'Something's off'* alarm bell we talked about doesn't just create a feeling; it creates an *urge*—a quick, automatic impulse to act. In the next chapter, we'll explore these urges and how they create our most self-sabotaging patterns.

You have just spent time noticing what happens inside you. Sensations, emotions, feelings. The whole internal weather report. And once you start paying attention, you realize your nervous system has been sending messages all along. Some are gentle nudges. Others feel more like a toddler with a whistle who found the volume button.

But here is the interesting part. All of that inner activity is not random. Your sensations show up for a reason. Your emotions are trying to get your attention. Your feelings are doing their best to make sense of the commotion. Together, they are pointing you toward something important.

A need.

Most of us are not taught to look there. We are taught to power through. To be fine. To react quickly. To just "deal with it." But your inner world is much more practical than that. It is not trying to overwhelm you. It is trying to help you. It is saying, "Hey, something matters here. Can you check on this?"

And this is where the next part of the work begins.

Because once you understand what your body and heart are asking for, communication starts to shift. You move from reacting to responding. From guessing to knowing. From hoping your partner will read your mind to actually giving them something to work with.

So as we move into the next chapter, we are going to talk about needs. What they really are. Why they matter so much in your relationship. And how naming your needs turns down the static and turns up the connection.

Think of this as learning a new language. One where your sensations begin the sentence, your emotions add context, your feelings offer color, and your needs finish the thought in a way your partner can finally understand.

Welcome to the part where things start to make more sense.

"Every criticism, judgment, diagnosis, and expression of anger is the tragic expression of an unmet need."

- MARSHALL B. ROSENBERG
(Nonviolent Communication)

CHAPTER 6

Needs

At the core of who you are is a set of universal needs, the stuff that keeps you feeling alive, connected, and sane. These aren't luxuries or signs that you're too sensitive. They're the foundation of your emotional health and your relationships. Every single emotion you feel, every urge that bubbles up, every decision you make is your system's way of saying, *"Hey, something matters here."*

When your needs are met, your body knows it. You exhale. You soften. You feel safe and steady. But when they're not, your body becomes an alarm system. Your chest tightens. Your thoughts race. Your shoulders tense. It's the emotional equivalent of a smoke detector saying, *"Pay attention."*

These needs run in the background of everything you do, whether you are conscious of them or not. They shape your moods, your reactions, and the ways you reach for or retreat from your partner. Learning to name and honor them is not selfish. It is how you build the kind of connection that lasts.

I remember learning about Maslow's Hierarchy of Needs back in college. It explains how our basic needs for food, sleep, and safety take priority before we can fully focus on things like love, purpose, or creativity.

Among the most basic universal needs are:

- ▶ Food
- ▶ Water
- ▶ Sleep

▶ Shelter
▶ Safety

All of your energy goes toward survival at this level. When one layer of needs is met, your system relaxes enough to consider the next. This is also true in relationships. When you do not feel emotionally secure, it is hard to relax into joy, play, or adventure. Your nervous system wants balance and the felt sense that you are safe with your person.

If you have ever been hangry, you know what unmet needs can do. This is why it is wise to think twice before starting a difficult conversation with someone who is tired or hungry.

Relationships are designed to help meet each other's needs. When they work well, they energize and comfort you. When they struggle, it hurts. No matter your story or personality, we all share core relational needs. When these needs are met, you feel secure and close to your partner.

When they are not met, frustration and anxiety often rise. These sensations and feelings are signals that something needs your attention.

Common Relationship Needs:
Emotional needs

▶ Love
▶ Kindness
▶ Validation
▶ Understanding
▶ Intimacy
▶ Freedom
▶ Empathy
▶ Respect
▶ Compassion
▶ Growth
▶ Shared Purpose

Safety and Stability

- ▶ Prioritization
- ▶ Support
- ▶ Trust
- ▶ Encouragement
- ▶ Celebration
- ▶ Loyalty

Social Needs

- ▶ Autonomy
- ▶ Belonging
- ▶ Teamwork
- ▶ Communication
- ▶ Shared Values
- ▶ Enjoyment
- ▶ Playfulness
- ▶ Individuality
- ▶ Intellectual Stimulation

Physical Needs

- ▶ Affection
- ▶ Sex
- ▶ Closeness
- ▶ Touch

Think about a time when you felt uneasy in your relationship. Maybe you felt unheard or unappreciated. That discomfort was not random. It was a signal. Emotions often help reveal an unmet need. But sometimes it is hard to distinguish what you truly need from what you simply want.

Let's explore that difference.

Needs and Wants: Understanding What Drives Us

Needs are universal. Every human has them. Safety, belonging, respect, comfort, connection, autonomy. These needs are often abstract. You cannot hold belonging in your hands, but you can certainly feel when you have it and when you do not.

Because needs are foundational, they are non-negotiable. When a need is unmet, your well-being shifts. You may feel anxious, disconnected, overwhelmed, or insecure. Needs shape your emotional balance and the overall health of your relationship.

Wants are different. A want is a specific way you prefer to meet a need. Wants add comfort and enjoyment, but they are not essential for emotional survival. If a want goes unmet, you may feel disappointed, but your sense of security remains intact.

Here are a few examples:

- Reliable transportation is a **need**. A new car is a **want**.
- Emotional safety is a **need**. Agreement on every issue is a **want**.
- Rest is a **need**. Sleeping in on weekends is a **want**.
- Connection is a **need**. Constant texting is a **want**.

People differ in their wants. The needs are the same.

Needs Are the Same. Wants Are Where Couples Differ

Usually, partners share the same needs. Where they differ is in how they try to meet those needs. That how is what we often call wants or strategies.

If your need is connection, your want might be long walks, meaningful conversations, or shared adventures.

If your partner's need is also connection, their want might be cuddling, quiet evenings, or working on a project together.

The need is universal and abstract.
The wants are personal and concrete.

Most conflict happens when couples cling to a specific want and lose sight of the need underneath. Once you come back to the need, collaboration and creativity become possible.

How This Shows Up in Real Life

Taylor walked in the door after a long day, shoulders up near their ears, breathing like someone who has just sprinted through an airport. Before they even had a chance to put down their bag, Sam appeared with a piece of paper and a worried look.

"Can you help me figure out this bill? Something looks wrong."
Taylor snapped. "Can I at least get inside before you bring me a problem?"

Sam went quiet. Taylor felt the familiar wave of guilt that follows the thought, *I wish I could take that back.* Time moved on anyway, and neither knew how to bridge the space that opened.

Later that evening, Taylor finally slowed down enough to notice what had happened inside their body. The irritability, the sharp tone, the automatic shut-down. None of it was about Sam or the bill. It was about Taylor's very real need for transition time after work, a few quiet minutes to become human again.

Taylor said, "When I came home earlier, I felt overwhelmed. I need a little time to settle before I can switch into anything else. When I snapped, I imagine it felt dismissive."

Sam nodded. "I was anxious about the bill. I think I reached for you to calm myself down. I didn't dial in to what you needed when you walked in."

And here is the important part. They did not solve the bill. They did not create a new household policy about greeting rituals. What changed everything was just naming what was underneath. Taylor needed a transition buffer between work and home. Sam needed reassurance. Once those needs were out in the open, the tension eased. Understanding drifted back into the room. Their energy softened, not because they fixed anything, but because they finally saw each other clearly again.

Why This Matters

When you can say:
"I felt overwhelmed when I walked in, and I need a little time to settle before I can engage."

instead of:
"You always come at me the second I walk in the door."

The entire conversation shifts. You move from tension to clarity, from guessing to understanding.

Needs bring you closer.

Wants help you choose how to meet those needs.
Flexibility keeps the relationship strong.

Naming your needs without locking them to a single strategy creates room for both of you to breathe and reconnect. It opens the door to understanding, even when nothing is solved. And that is one of the core skills of wholehearted communication.

Understanding and Meeting Each Other's Needs

One of the greatest gifts you can offer your partner is learning what they need and how they experience those needs being met. The Five Love Languages became popular for this exact reason. It helped couples see that we often try to meet each other's needs using our own preferred strategies.

Chapman identified five common strategies for meeting the universal need for love and connection: words of affirmation, quality time, physical touch, gifts, and acts of service. Each one is a different pathway that satisfies the universal need for love and connection.

Couples often discover they've been missing each other not because they lack love, but because they express it differently. One person may show love through doing. The other may long for uninterrupted time together. Both are giving love. They are just using different strategies.

When you separate the need from the strategy, something shifts. You become less rigid, less defensive, and more willing to explore new possibilities. The focus moves from my way to our way.

Try asking:

- ▶ When do you feel most loved and connected?
- ▶ What helps you feel safe and valued?
- ▶ What is one thing I could do to help you feel more supported?

The more you understand what meets your partner's needs, the easier it becomes to create a relationship where both of you feel fulfilled.

The Language of Needs

Recognizing your needs is only half the work. Communicating them clearly is the other half. When you focus too much on a specific strategy, your request can sound like a demand, which often leads to defensiveness or withdrawal.

When you express your needs with clarity and vulnerability, without tying them to a single method, you create space for collaboration.

Consider the difference:

- ▶ **Strategy/Want-focused:** "Will you put your phone down while I'm talking?"
- ▶ **Need-focused:** "I need to feel like a priority. I would love to have your attention when you are available."

The first statement comes across as a demand, which might trigger resistance or defensiveness. The second, however, expresses a real need (feeling like a priority) and invites a solution without dictating exactly how it should happen. It opens the door for your partner to engage in a way that works for both of you.

A Practice in Vulnerability

Communicating your needs effectively takes practice. It requires vulnerability, patience, and a willingness to let go of control over how your needs are met. If you're used to staying silent about your needs or expressing them through frustration rather than directness, this shift may feel uncomfortable at first. The more you practice, the easier it is.

Here are a few guiding principles for expressing needs in a way that fosters connection:

- ▶ **Be clear and direct.**
- ▶ **Focus on the feeling, not the strategy**. Instead of saying, "You never plan dates," try, "I feel most connected when we spend intentional time together."
- ▶ **Use "I" statements.** Instead of, "You never listen to me," try, "I feel unheard when we talk about important things, and I'd love to feel more connected in our conversations."
- ▶ **Make space for your partner's perspective.** After expressing your need, invite a response: "How does that sound to you?"

Your needs are the foundation of your emotional and physical well-being. Understanding and honoring them is necessary for building happy relationships. By distinguishing between needs and wants, recognizing satisfiers and strategies, and communicating with clarity and vulnerability, you set the stage for deeper connection and mutual fulfillment.

Quiz: Distinguishing Needs, Wants, and Strategies

For each statement below, decide whether it represents a **need**, a **want/strategy**. If it's a want or strategy, rewrite it to reflect the need behind it.

1. "I want you to spend more time with me on the weekends."

2. "I need to feel appreciated for my work in this relationship."

3. "I want you to compliment me more often."

4. "I want to spend our date night at a fancy restaurant."

5. "I need to feel emotionally safe when discussing difficult topics."

6. "I wish you'd send me good morning texts every day."

7. "I want us to go on more vacations together."

8. "I want you to agree with me when we argue."

9. "I need space to process my emotions before we continue our conversation."

10. "I want you to help more around the house."

Answer Key

1. **"I want you to spend more time with me on the weekends."**

▶ **Want/Strategy**

▶ **Reframe:** "I need quality time to feel connected with you."

2. **"I need to feel appreciated for the work I do in this relationship."**

▶ **Need** (No correction needed)

3. **"I want you to compliment me more often."**

▶ **Want/Strategy**

▶ **Reframe:** "I need to feel valued and appreciated."

4. **"I want to spend our date night at a fancy restaurant."**

▶ **Want/Strategy**

▶ **Reframe:** "I need special time with you to nurture our connection."

5. **"I need to feel emotionally safe when discussing difficult topics."**

▶ **Need** (No correction needed)

6. **"I wish you'd send me good morning texts daily."**

▶ **Want/Strategy**

▶ **Reframe:** "I need reassurance and connection to start my day positively."

7. **"I want us to go on more vacations together."**

▶ **Want/Strategy**

▶ **Reframe:** "I need shared experiences that allow us to deepen our bond."

8. **"I want you to agree with me when we argue."**

   ▶ **Want/Strategy**

   ▶ **Reframe:** "I need understanding and validation of my perspective."

9. **"I need space to process my emotions before we continue our conversation."**

   ▶ **Need** (No correction needed)

10. **"I want you to help more around the house."**

   ▶ **Want/Strategy**

   ▶ **Reframe:** "I need to feel supported in maintaining our shared responsibilities."

"When we are in survival mode, we cannot connect. The brain cannot do both at once."

– DAN SIEGEL

CHAPTER 7

Self-Protection

Have you ever noticed how some interactions with your partner just feel easy? Like you can breathe deeper, laugh a little louder, and let yourself be fully seen? That's not an accident. It's your nervous system picking up cues that say, *Hey, it's safe to be here.*

Believe it or not, your nervous system has a pretty simple filing system. It puts every experience into one of two folders: *safe* or *dangerous.* When it senses safety, your best self shows up open, playful, relaxed, and trusting. That's when connection happens effortlessly.

But when something feels off, even slightly, your body shifts without asking for permission. A look, a tone, a silence, or a sudden change in energy can send the message: *This might not be safe.* And in that instant, connection gives way to self-protection. Because your nervous system won't let you do both at the same time. You're either protecting yourself or connecting with each other.

Cues of Safety

Think of cues of safety, a term widely used by Polyvagal Theory educator Deb Dana, as your nervous system's 'green lights.' They're the subtle (and sometimes not-so-subtle) signals that tell your body, *You're okay here. You can let your guard down.* These cues indicate that you can be open, playful, and engage with others safely.

When your brain picks up these messages, it quietly says, *All systems go. Enjoy yourself.* That's when your shoulders drop, you exhale, and you feel a sense of ease. These instances often don't come from grand gestures but from the small, everyday signs that you're seen, valued, and emotionally safe.

Here are some examples of cues that help us feel safe and connected:

- ▶ Being celebrated
- ▶ Laughter
- ▶ Affection
- ▶ Eye contact
- ▶ Active listening
- ▶ Validation
- ▶ Support
- ▶ Positive feedback
- ▶ Kindness
- ▶ Apologies
- ▶ Playfulness
- ▶ Accountability
- ▶ Encouragement
- ▶ Being prioritized

Each of these cues invites your body to relax, your heart to open, and your relationship to deepen. Unsurprisingly, these behaviors also build trust. When our system receives reliable cues of safety from others, we begin to predict that this is how they are, that we can count on them to be safe people.

Cues of Danger

On the flip side, *cues of danger* are your nervous system's flashing red lights. Sometimes they're subtle, sometimes loud, but either way, your body interprets them as: *Something isn't right. Be on alert.* These cues activate anxiety, fear, or hypervigilance and prepare your body to respond to a perceived threat.

Here are some common cues of danger in relationships:

- ▶ Turning away
- ▶ Not listening
- ▶ Invalidation
- ▶ Stonewalling
- ▶ Disinterest
- ▶ Withholding affection
- ▶ Constant criticism
- ▶ Lack of accountability
- ▶ Blame
- ▶ Controlling behavior
- ▶ Preoccupation

When a cue of danger is detected, your nervous system releases chemical instructions that shift your entire physiological state. These reactions are often tied to old experiences, like a look, a tone, or a phrase that once caused pain. Real or not, your body doesn't wait for confirmation; it acts fast.

Once you register a cue of danger, your body is flooded with chemicals that create uncomfortable sensations:

- ▶ Your heart rate speeds up
- ▶ Your breathing gets shallow or rapid
- ▶ Blood flows to your arms and legs so you can fight, flee, or freeze
- ▶ Sugar floods your bloodstream and revs up your energy
- ▶ Stress hormones like cortisol and adrenaline surge
- ▶ Your thinking brain takes a back seat to your survival brain

When this happens, your urge to self-protect takes center stage. And no matter how much you want to stay connected, your body is saying, *This is not safe. Defend or retreat.*

Our automatic survival instincts serve two purposes:

1. Motivate actions to satisfy our needs
2. Protect us from the threat of danger

To experience Wholehearted Communication, you must shift into a place of openness and out of self-protection.

The Protector vs. The Connected Self

Emotional dysregulation occurs when the intensity of your internal experience becomes overwhelming, and your nervous system can no longer maintain balance. In this state, your ability to stay grounded and present decreases, and a part of you steps in to help. I call this part your Protector.

The Protector's job is to keep you safe, not connected. It steps in when your system senses danger, doing whatever it must to help you regain control. Protectors do not erase love. They simply put love on pause until safety returns.

The term Protector is also used in Internal Family Systems, a model created by Dr. Richard Schwartz. While I am not using the word in the technical therapeutic sense that IFS teaches, the everyday idea does overlap with IFS concepts. IFS describes many Protectors, each with its own role and personality. In Wholehearted Communication, you do not need to sort out multiple parts. It is enough to notice the protective pattern that shows up when you feel overwhelmed or unsafe in your relationship.

The idea of the Connected Self is also influenced by IFS. In that model, the Self is described with qualities such as calm, clarity, compassion, curiosity, confidence, courage, creativity, and connectedness. In this book, the Connected Self is simply the part of you that can stay open, curious, grounded, and present with your partner. It is the version of you that can listen and respond with intention instead of reacting from fear or hurt. It is the part of you your partner fell in love with.

When stress chemicals flood your system, it can feel as if your body has dosed itself with a powerful drug. Biology takes the wheel. You might say things you do not mean or act in ways you later regret. That is how strongly your body is wired to protect you from danger.

When the Protector takes charge, it temporarily pushes the Connected Self out of the conversation. Learning to notice which part of you is leading in any given moment is the first step toward regulation and connection.

A simple way to build this awareness is to name what you feel in your body as it happens. You might say, "My heart is pounding. I feel a little nauseous. My chest is tight, and my hands are warm." Naming your sensations helps you stay grounded and keeps you from getting swept away by the stories your mind wants to create.

Alarm System

Your Emotional Guidance System (EGS) acts as an internal alarm, constantly scanning your environment for potential threats. It prompts fight, flight, freeze, fix, fawn, or flop responses to protect your well-being and survival. We looked at these earlier in the book, and here is where you begin to see how they operate within your communication. These responses are not character flaws. They are your Protector doing its job the only way it knows how.

Efficiency Over Precision

Your brain does not interpret every situation from scratch. That would take too much time and energy. Instead, it relies on shortcuts based on past experiences. Most of the time, these shortcuts are helpful and allow you to move through the world more efficiently.

But sometimes they backfire.

If your childhood home was filled with volatility, your brain may have learned that raised voices mean danger. Then, as an adult, even a passionate or harmless discussion might feel threatening, triggering an old survival response.

On the other hand, if raised voices were common and did not signal danger, you may associate them with energy, familiarity, or even connection.

Your nervous system is always working to protect you. But it does not always get it right. It reacts based on what used to be true, not necessarily what is true now.

Home Country

We all grow up with different filters, shaped by the environments that teach us what "normal" looks like. This is your home country, the land of the people who raised you.

I like to think of relationships as an international event. It is two cultures coming together, each with its own language, customs, and expectations. Even if you and your partner grew up in the same neighborhood or went to the same school, your emotional cultures are still different. Each home creates its own atmosphere, coauthored by everyone who shares the space, including parents, siblings, and others who played a role in your early years.

In some home countries, communication is loud, fast, and full of overlapping voices. People might call it passionate. In others, it is quiet and restrained, where feelings are private and rarely expressed. Most of us fall somewhere in between, shaped by the unspoken rules we absorbed about how to talk, listen, disagree, and show love.

Over time, your home country becomes the lens through which you see the world. It defines what feels safe, what feels threatening, and how you expect people to behave. Those early patterns are stored in your nervous system and quietly guide how you relate to others.

Your nervous system is like a home alarm system, always running in the background, scanning for cues of safety or danger. As you move through life, everything you experience is filtered through the culture of your home country.

Conflicts

Conflicts happen between two people when one or both of you register a cue of danger. The more intense the conflict feels, the deeper the hurt tends to be. And the deeper the hurt, the deeper the roots of your pain, often reaching all the way back to childhood.

When your nervous system keeps encountering familiar pain, it starts to build a case. *This is how it always is. This is how it always will be. You will always be misunderstood. Always be less important. Always be left. Never be good enough.* Whatever your early pain was, your body remembers.

That is why some conflicts feel so big. Because they are. Not just in the present, but in what they awaken from your past.

When Protectors Collide

Understanding your own nervous system is just as important as recognizing your partner's Protector. Every relationship is a dance between two nervous systems, each shaped by its own history, triggers, and ways of staying safe. When one person becomes activated, the other often follows. Before you know it, both of you are reacting instead of connecting.

When your partner is activated, it is similar to interacting with someone under the influence of drugs or alcohol. The chemicals released by the nervous system during perceived danger push the body into survival mode, whether the threat is real or not.

When the nervous system floods the body with stress hormones like adrenaline and cortisol, it temporarily changes how we think, feel, and respond. It is like being under the influence of your body's own chemistry. When your partner is flooded, their ability to think clearly and communicate effectively is compromised. This is not a sign of weakness or dysfunction. It is biology.

That is why it is so important to remember that what appears to be a character flaw is often just the nervous system doing its job a little too well.

The first step toward staying connected is noticing when either of you is in a heightened state. Ask yourself, "Am I interacting with their Connected Self or their Protector?"

This fluid movement between protection and connection is part of being human. You cannot fully be in both at the same time. When your nervous system senses threat, protection steps in and connection fades. When safety returns, connection naturally reemerges.

That awareness opens the door to empathy. Instead of reacting to the behavior, you can respond to what is underneath it. This is where you can remind yourself:

"My partner is reacting to something that feels threatening. Right now, I'm no longer face-to-face with their Connected Self. I'm face-to-face with their Protector."

What creates the most disconnection is when your Protector comes out to meet your partner's Protector.

Over time, as you both get better at noticing who is running the show, your relationship begins to shift. Instead of getting caught in the same old reaction loops, you start to build understanding, take responsibility, repair more easily, and create stronger connections.

With Wholehearted Communication, the hope is to notice these shifts sooner and stay longer in the safety of real connection, where trust takes root, healing begins, and love has room to grow.

Compassion Is Not Permission

Understanding where a partner's emotional reactivity comes from is not the same as excusing their hurtful behavior.

When someone is activated, their nervous system reacts not just to what is happening now, but also to a backlog of unresolved pain. The greater the past wounds, the greater the emotional reactivity tends to be. When someone grows up in a home where safety, predictability, or caring engagement were missing, their nervous system learns to stay on alert. It becomes finely tuned to pick up on danger.

People who've lived through trauma, abuse, or neglect often develop nervous systems that react fast and strong to anything that feels threatening. Even something as small as a tone of voice, a facial expression, or a pause can sound the alarm. The body moves into protection before the mind has time to decide what's real.

That doesn't mean something is wrong with them. It means their system did its job. It learned how to survive. What once protected them can now make it hard to stay calm and connected when there's no real threat. Healing begins when we notice these reactions, thank our Protector for trying to help, and remind ourselves that we're safe enough to choose a new response.

Instead of shaming your partner for their reactivity, the work is to understand it, accept that it's there, and then team up against the behaviors that create disconnection and cause pain. That means recognizing self-protective behavior as a learned survival response, not a character flaw. It means holding space for your partner's healing while still maintaining your own boundaries.

This only works when your partner is willing to take responsibility, repair the harm, and continue making changes when they are no longer activated.

Some behaviors are not acceptable, regardless of history:

- ▶ Physical violence or threats of harm
- ▶ Cruel, demeaning name-calling
- ▶ Repeated verbal attacks meant to shame, belittle, or control
- ▶ Gaslighting or consistent manipulation

> ▶ Persistent refusal to acknowledge the impact or take responsibility for their words or actions

> ▶ Emotional abandonment or stonewalling as a chronic pattern

These dynamics are especially common when unresolved trauma or personality disorders are present. While these experiences may explain why someone behaves the way they do, they never justify continuing that harm. You can hold compassion and boundaries at the same time. In fact, maintaining your self-respect and boundaries is often the supportive response your partner needs in order to heal.

In healthy relationships, both partners take responsibility for how their past shows up in the present. They do the work to repair, to grow, and to create a future that feels safe and connected. You are not meant to be the target of your partner's pain. You are meant to be their partner in healing.

The Power of the Pause

Every time you notice yourself slipping into a defensive behavior, pause. Think of it as your built-in upgrade button. You get a moment to shift out of automatic pilot and into something more intentional.

The pause is what helps you sort out who is speaking inside you. Is this your Protector jumping in, fast and loud, or the version of you that goes silent and shuts down, trying to keep you safe? Or is this your Connected Self, the one who takes a breath, looks around, and chooses a response instead of a reaction? Protectors react quickly because fear feels urgent. The Connected Self moves slowly because love is not in a hurry.

A pause does more than interrupt the ineffective interaction. It gives you a chance to look underneath the surface. Are you reacting to an old story or a familiar fear? Is a well-worn pattern sensing abandonment, criticism, or rejection before anything has even happened? Later in this book, we will talk about how your attachment style shapes these patterns. For now, it is enough to notice that when something feels threatening, your Protector shows up fast, doing what it has always done to keep you safe.

When you pause, you create space between the trigger and your next move. That space is where intention lives. It is where you can choose a response that reflects who you want to be in the moment, not just who you have been in the past.

We all bring a Protector into our relationships. This part of you learned how to handle fear, rejection, shame, or vulnerability. It is not bad. It is even necessary. But the Protector's job is to defend, not to love. When you notice it taking the lead, you have a choice: keep defending, or pause and ask yourself, "What would love do here?"

"You are doing the best you can, and you can do better."

– MARSHA LINEHAN

CHAPTER 8

Urges, Bumblebees, and Turtles

So far on this journey toward self-awareness, we've looked at the stories we tell ourselves, the emotions that rise up, and the sensations those emotions create in our bodies. Those sensations aren't random. They exist to signal that something matters and to push you toward action.

That push shows up as an urge, the quick and automatic impulse to do something that will ease discomfort. It might feel like the need to lash out, shut down, walk away, fix something, or defend yourself. These impulses aren't bad. They're your body's way of trying to protect you and bring relief.

Once you're emotionally activated, your nervous system calls on your Protector, the part of you that learned how to stay safe in difficult moments. The Protector's job is to restore a sense of safety, often by relying on old patterns that once worked well. That's why urges can feel so powerful. Your Protector still believes you need saving, even when you're safe enough now to choose another way.

Maybe as a child, withdrawing was your Protector's way of keeping you safe when things felt chaotic at home. Or perhaps your Protector learned that pushing harder, speaking louder, and demanding attention was the only way to feel seen. Back then, these strategies served a purpose. They helped you survive the emotional terrain of your childhood. But what worked then can backfire now, especially in your closest relationships. The same protective urges that once kept you safe can now create distance instead of closeness.

Let's look at how these automatic urges typically show up in relationships.

Imagine you send your partner an important message and hours go by without a reply. You feel tension in your chest and stomach, and your mind starts spinning stories: *Are they ignoring me? Do they even care?*

Before you realize it, your body pushes you toward a familiar reaction. Maybe you fire off an angry text demanding an explanation, or you shut down and convince yourself you don't care. Neither response is wrong or bad. They're simply your system's way of trying to relieve discomfort, using the same protective patterns that once helped you feel safe.

Our urges are driven by a desire to ease the discomfort of difficult emotions, not by a plan to create closeness. That's why they so often send the opposite message. We reach for connection but end up pushing it away.

When it comes to relationships, these protective urges tend to move in two directions. Some of us react by leaning in and trying harder to reconnect. Others pull back to find calm and safety. Both directions make sense when you understand what your nervous system is trying to do.

These patterns are also well described in attachment theory, first developed by John Bowlby and later expanded for couples by Sue Johnson. Attachment theory which explains how our early experiences shape the way we seek closeness, handle distress, and protect ourselves in relationships.

Turtles and Bumblebees

Now let's look at how your Protector tends to behave in relationships. I call these patterns Turtle and Bumblebee behaviors. They show up most clearly when emotions run high and your nervous system is trying to keep you safe.

The dance between a Turtle and a Bumblebee reveals more about communication than any label ever could. The Bumblebee's instinct is to move toward connection, to protest, insist, or demand. The Turtle's instinct is to pull away, to retreat, avoid, or minimize. Both are trying to restore a sense of safety, just in opposite ways.

Sometimes it is not one Turtle and one Bumblebee at all. Sometimes it is two Turtles quietly avoiding tension, two Bumblebees chasing connection at full speed, or a pair of Turtlebees doing a little of both. *Turtlebees* are people whose nervous systems switch between the two instincts. In one moment they pull away to find safety, and in the next they move in fast to reclaim closeness. It can feel confusing, both for them and for their partner, but the pattern is simply a sign that their system learned to use both strategies at different times in their life.

You do not need to map this onto full attachment styles to understand it. What matters here is the dance. Every protective move is either a pull inward or a push outward. Once you can spot those two movements in yourself and in your partner, the whole pattern becomes easier to understand and much easier to shift.

Recognizing these patterns is not about judgment. It is about awareness. When you can see your Turtle or your Bumblebee, or both, stepping in to protect you, you create the opportunity to invite your Connected Self back into the conversation. And that is where real change begins.

Bumblebee Behavior: Pushing to Engage

This is the instinct to push for resolution, fight for connection, and make sure your voice is heard. The Bumblebee's Protector moves outward, buzzing with energy, seeking reassurance, and demanding engagement. It tries to make things unfold in a way that feels safe and predictable.

When this urge takes over, you might find yourself:

▸ Raising your voice to make sure your partner is listening.
▸ Repeating yourself, hoping they will finally understand.

- ▶ Pressing for an answer right now because the uncertainty feels unbearable.
- ▶ Becoming critical or blaming, convinced things will change if you just point it out enough.

This response is rooted in a fear of disconnection. When your partner feels distant or unresponsive, the Protector sounds the alarm and tells you to push harder so you will not be left alone. The impulse makes complete sense. It is your nervous system trying to reestablish safety through contact.

The challenge is that while the pushing comes from a longing for closeness, it often has the opposite effect. The intensity can overwhelm your partner's nervous system, triggering their Protector to retreat. The more they pull away, the stronger your urge becomes to chase connection.

When you can recognize that cycle in the moment, you create space for your Connected Self to step in, to pause, breathe, and reach for understanding instead of control.

Turtle Behavior: Withdrawing or Avoiding

The Turtle's approach is to seek safety by withdrawing into their shell. Turtles have an instinct to go inward, retreat, and focus on what they can control. Unlike the Bumblebee, everything slows down for the Turtle. And when the overwhelm becomes too much, they may go numb or completely shut down.

When this urge takes over, you might find yourself:

- ▶ Go quiet or give one-word answers to end the conversation.
- ▶ Leave the room to avoid conflict.
- ▶ Change the subject or make a joke to deflect.
- ▶ Say whatever your partner wants to hear just to end the tension.
- ▶ Convince yourself it is not worth the fight and suppress your feelings.

This response often comes from a deep discomfort with conflict. When emotions run high, your nervous system sounds the alarm: *This is too much. Get out. Stay safe.* So you retreat, believing that avoiding the conflict will make it go away.

Over time, Turtles often develop a mindset that the best way to not get hurt is to not need anyone. But just as the Bumblebee's instinct to push outward can backfire, the Turtle's instinct to turn inward can too.

When you "Turtle down," your partner may feel alone, especially if they tend to respond with Bumblebee behaviors. The more a Turtle withdraws, the more a Bumblebee pushes. The harder the Bumblebee pushes, the further the Turtle retreats. Not every couple falls into this pattern, but it is one of the most common dynamics I see. What matters is learning how these self-protective patterns interact.

When one person withdraws and the other pursues, it becomes an emotional game of hide-and-seek that leaves both people frustrated and disconnected.

Back to the unanswered text. If the Turtle sent the message, their instinct might be to let it go, avoiding any potential conflict. But under that avoidance, resentment can quietly grow. The Bumblebee, on the other hand, may either feel hurt that the Turtle seems unconcerned, or be unaware that the Turtle is hurt at all.

To be clear, neither approach to self-protection is better or worse than the other. Both are attempts to stay safe, and both are ineffective in creating connection. Turtles often believe they are taking the high road by avoiding conflict, staying calm, and being logical, but in reality, it is a quieter form of dysregulation that leads to the same outcome: disconnection.

Bumblebees, on the other hand, often feel unheard or dismissed because of the intensity they bring, which results in the same painful distance.

Why does this happen?

Connecting Your Past to Your Present

It all comes down to how your nervous system handles threat and safety. When something feels off between you and your partner, your brain does not stop to analyze what is really happening. It reacts, often faster than your conscious mind can catch up.

For a Bumblebee, distance feels dangerous. The nervous system sounds the alarm and says, *Do something. Close the gap. Fix this now.* So you move toward your partner, hoping that connection will calm you down.

For a Turtle, intensity feels dangerous. The nervous system sends a different message: *This is too much. Slow it down. Get away before you lose control.* So you move back, hoping that space will bring relief.

Both are searching for safety, but they use opposite strategies to find it. The Bumblebee feels safe through closeness. The Turtle feels safe through distance. Neither is wrong. Each is simply trying to soothe an activated nervous system that is saying, *Something here does not feel safe.*

Here is where the trouble begins. The Bumblebee's push feels like pressure to the Turtle. The Turtle's retreat feels like rejection to the Bumblebee. The more one pushes, the more the other withdraws. The dance becomes automatic, and neither partner is choosing the steps anymore.

When this cycle takes over, both people feel misunderstood. The Bumblebee thinks, *If I could just explain myself better, they would get it.* The Turtle thinks, *If they would just calm down, I could listen.* Both are trying to feel safe, yet both are missing each other's signals.

The goal is not to eliminate your Protector, but to acknowledge it. When you can recognize your Protector's instinct to keep you safe, you create a little space between the urge and the action. In that space, your Connected Self has a chance to step in, to choose a response that reflects who you are now rather than what once kept you safe.

When it comes to urges, we are not very creative. When certain emotions get triggered, we tend to respond in the same predictable ways. Over time, the nervous system learns what to expect and jumps ahead to protect us.

But in relationships, that shortcut becomes a trap. Once your body recognizes the early steps of a familiar conflict, it races ahead. You start reacting to what you *expect* will happen next instead of what is happening now. I call this the "Here We Go Again" effect.

The Conflict Accelerator

Every couple has what I call the Here-We-Go-Again (HWGA) effect. It's that moment when you are convinced you know what's coming next, and you react as if it's already happening. When you start responding to what you anticipate instead of what is unfolding in front of you, the HWGA effect can turn a small spark into a full-fledged fire.

Let's look at this interaction between Morgan and Jade.

Morgan poked their head into Jade's home office to ask for help holding a ladder so Morgan could finish power-washing the tallest peak of the house. Jade said, "Yes, please wait for me; I need to send one last email, and I'll be right out."

Twelve minutes later, Jade closed their laptop and headed outside to find Morgan. On the way, Jade noticed a cluster of weeds in the flower bed on the side of the house. As Jade bent down to pick them, Morgan rounded the corner to find Jade bent over the flower bed.

Morgan stopped abruptly, shifted their weight to one leg, and crossed both arms tightly across their chest. Upset, Morgan asked sarcastically, "Really?"

Jade was caught off guard, and their heart started racing. Instinctively, Jade smiled and said, "Hey there, I've come to help."

Morgan lowered their eyebrows, curled their lip, and continued, "Looks to me like you've got better things to do than help me!"

Oh shit, thought Jade, *Here we go again*.

Morgan felt an immediate flood of sensations. Their body reacted before their mind could catch up. Jade's detour to the flower bed triggered an old, familiar feeling that had nothing to do with the weeds or the ladder.

In our session, Morgan recognized that there was no logic behind that reaction. This is common. Our emotional responses rarely make sense until we slow down enough to connect the dots.

When I asked Morgan, "When have you felt this way before, as far back as you can remember?" they recalled spending long hours alone as a child while their mother, often intoxicated, forgot to pick them up from school or make dinner. Over time, Morgan learned to anticipate being let down and to rely on anger to get attention. Anger, in that environment, worked.

Jade's behavior was nothing like Morgan's mother's, but the feeling it sparked was the same.

Emotions Cannot Be Understood with Logic

Seeing Jade bent over the flower bed triggered a deep feeling of insignificance that Morgan's body recognized instantly. Without any conscious thought, Morgan's nervous system sounded the alarm and launched a protective response.

These urges are your body's way of saying, *I have been here before, and I know how to survive this.* But what once protected you in childhood can quietly sabotage connection in your adult relationships if you do not notice and interrupt those automatic reactions.

Meanwhile, Jade's nervous system went through its own activation. Caught off guard by Morgan's tone, Jade froze, overwhelmed by the familiar sense of being misunderstood. In that instant, Jade decided there was no way to fix it, and silence felt safer than trying.

The Pattern Is the Problem

How you interact with the people you love becomes automatic over time. When someone says or does x, you respond with y. Eventually, they do not even have to say or do x anymore. Your body simply recognizes the pattern and jumps straight to y.

That is how conflict speeds up. The HWGA moment is like hitting the fast-forward button on your relationship. Everything moves faster. You skip over parts. You jump to conclusions and start reacting to things that have not even happened yet.

Morgan felt dismissed. Jade felt defeated. Neither one was wrong. They were both caught in an old dance that began long before they met each other.

The issue was not Morgan or Jade. It was the pattern between their Protectors, the familiar choreography of two nervous systems trying, in their own ways, to feel safe, even when there was no real threat.

Updating the Automated Programming

Here is a small exercise inspired by Dr. Sue Johnson's work. She teaches that every couple has a dance they fall into during conflict. Not the fun, date-night kind of dance. More like the one you wander into accidentally, where each partner moves in ways that make perfect sense in the moment but somehow keep stepping on the other's toes.

This exercise helps you see that dance clearly.

Think of a recent conflict and fill in the blanks below:

When they _____, I _____.
Then they _____, and I _____.
Then they _____, and I _____.

Do this gently. No judging, no scoring, no deciding who should have done what. You are simply naming the pattern, so it becomes visible.

When you see your dance on paper, something shifts. It stops feeling like chaos and starts looking like a sequence, a routine that you fall into without meaning to. And once you can see the routine, you can change it.

You realize that their move is not an attack. It is a reaction. Your move is not a flaw. It is a habit. And together, these habits create the steps that keep the two of you stuck.

Awareness gives you choice. Choice gives you new steps. And that is where compassion grows.

Jade and Morgan could see one another more clearly when they stopped looking for the logic in their interaction. Jade said, "I can see how it would feel like I didn't care about you and your safety on the ladder when you saw me picking weeds."

Without looking up, Morgan said, "I appreciate you acknowledging how that affected me, and I am sorry I overreacted. In my right mind, I know you have my back, but in those situations, I'm not in my right mind. I react so fast, and I don't even think."

Jade said, "I'm here for you, even when it seems I'm not."

Morgan reassured Jade, "And you are always more than good enough, even when my reactions might try to convince you otherwise."

Healing begins with understanding and repair. Your urges are shaped by the degree of danger or emotional activation you feel. The stronger the activation, the more intense the urge. Just like the sensations in your body, your urges follow a well-worn path, leading you to take specific actions to alleviate your inner discomfort.

When you can see through your partner's instinct to self-protect and pause before indulging your urge to react, you can slow things down and rework your dance. The goal is to outsmart your nervous system. Though it is doing its job and working hard to keep you safe, it is not always accurate.

Breaking the Cycle: From Reaction to Response

Self-protective urges like pushing for connection (Bumblebee) or pulling away for safety (Turtle) are deeply wired patterns. They exist to protect you, but when they run the show, they often lead to disconnection instead of resolution.

In the middle of a tough interaction, you will not always have the space to pause and reflect. That is okay. The work begins before the conflict. Start by noticing your pattern when things are calm. Learn what your Protector feels like in your body: the quick heartbeat, the urge to talk faster, the pull to walk away. When you can recognize those early signals, you can step in sooner and choose a different move.

If you are a Bumblebee, practice slowing your pace, softening your tone, or taking one slow breath before you speak. If you are a Turtle, practice staying present for ten more seconds, keeping eye contact, or letting your partner know you need a short break instead of disappearing.

These small shifts help you interrupt the Protector's automatic response and invite your Connected Self back into the conversation. Over time, this practice creates new pathways that lead to understanding instead of distance.

Whatever the urge, it is always an attempt to self-protect. Yet in love, self-protection creates distance where connection is needed most. Once you get good at recognizing your urges, the next step is noticing whether your choices create the outcomes you want. That's what we'll explore in the next chapter, *Effective Actions*.

"Out beyond ideas
of wrongdoing and
rightdoing, there is
a field. I'll meet
you there."

- RUMI

CHAPTER 9

Effective Actions

Conflict is natural when two people with different needs, fears, opinions, and histories are trying to build something real together. Research supports this. It's not whether you have conflict, but how you handle it that shapes the health of your connection.

Every conflict brings you to a crossroads. One path leads toward understanding and growth. The other leads toward distance and resentment. The trick is learning to slow down long enough to see that fork in the road before you take a turn you don't mean to.

In fact, as I write this, my wife and I are recovering from a disagreement where we missed that fork. It's true. We were discussing the purchase of a new property and had a disagreement about how we see things. The issue isn't the house.

We got that far.

The issue is how we make decisions. She processes all the pros and cons out loud. She goes back and forth, looking for clarity. She needs to hear it all out loud and get my input on whether or not I see the same concerns.

I, on the other hand, process internally. I gather data, do the research, and move quickly. She prefers to take her time and evaluate every angle.

As sure as I sit here typing, I can see the detour I missed, back when I expressed frustration with her worries. I should have recognized that her concerns weren't a hesitation about moving forward. They were her way of making sure we were doing the right thing. My *intention* was to signal I was ready to move, but the *impact* was that I made her feel dismissed and rushed.

I'm a Turtle, and when I get dysregulated, I tend to go inward the more she goes outward. But that's not effective communication. What she really needs is for me to use my words and help her understand what's going on inside of me so she can understand why I appear so insensitive to her concerns.

Like most couples, our hardest times are when our resilience is low or our stress is high. It's time for us to put it in reverse, find that fork in the road, and choose the path that leads back to repair and reconnection.

The question isn't if conflict will happen. The real question is whether we will use our conflict to bring us closer or push us apart.

The Goal: Intention and Impact Are the Same

This is the goal of effective communication. But as you've probably experienced, it's rarely that simple. Just because you say something doesn't mean it's heard, let alone understood as you intended.

Real communication is more than the exchange of words. It is about building connection. It happens when your intention aligns with your impact, when what you mean to share is what the other person actually hears and feels.

That kind of alignment takes the intention to speak clearly, listen without defensiveness, and stay curious rather than jumping to conclusions. When you show up this way, you create a space where both people can feel seen, heard, and valued.

That's where trust grows. That's where connection happens.

Although I've been doing this work professionally and in my own relationship for years, I still get it wrong. My nervous system takes over. I say the wrong thing. I shut down. I get defensive.

No amount of knowledge makes you immune to being human. I can't always override my biology when I'm activated, and neither can you. The goal isn't perfection. It's progress.

Progress means recognizing what's happening a little sooner and finding our way back to repair a little faster. That alone is growth. Because effective communication isn't about saying everything just right, it's about getting to the heart of what we need and being understood.

So why is this so hard? The gap between our intention and our impact is created by a few common problems.

Problem 1: We Argue About the "Story," Not the Feeling

Most relationship conflicts aren't about brand-new issues. They're usually about the same core hurts that keep showing up in different outfits. The stories change. The circumstances shift. But the feelings underneath? They're often painfully familiar.

Take a look at these four complaints one partner might have:

- ▶ "We never have time together."
- ▶ "You give most of your energy to work."
- ▶ "You're always on your phone."
- ▶ "You're happier to see the dog than you are to see me."

At first glance, they sound like different frustrations. But if you sit with them for a minute, you'll notice the thread that runs through all of them. It's not just about time, attention, or screen use. The deeper message is something like: *"I feel disconnected from you. I miss us. I feel unimportant."*

When you recognize the theme underneath the complaint, the whole conversation shifts. You're no longer fighting about the phone, the dog, or the calendar. You're talking about what matters: longing, closeness, and how to find your way back to each other.

Problem 2: We're Biologically Wired to Protect

Effective communication means naming what you're feeling and what you need with clarity and courage. Still, that's rarely where partners begin.

Our nervous system isn't wired for vulnerability. It's wired for safety. So, when something stings, it is not instinctive to pause and say, "Let me calmly share my emotions with you." More often, the automated response is to move into self-protection, fast.

Picture this:

- ▶ Your partner says something that hits a nerve. You hear it and immediately feel like your emotions don't matter.
- ▶ Your chest tightens. Your stomach flips. Your throat closes in.
- ▶ Your body is now responding to potential danger. You might react with a sharp edge: "Why do you always dismiss me?!" Or retreat into silence.

Underneath all that reaction, though, is something vulnerable. You want to feel loved. Valued. Seen.

The challenge is this: self-protective reactions send confusing signals. In fact, it's common to react in the exact opposite way of how you're feeling. If you feel small and hurt, you might react with big hot anger. If you feel anxious and concerned, you might react with a calm, cool demeanor.

Instead of reaching for your partner with vulnerability, you end up pushing them away. What gets communicated isn't "I'm hurting and need connection," but "I'm frustrated, disappointed, or shutting down." The intention is to protect yourself, but the impact is to create more distance.

When you criticize, withdraw, or lash out, the message that lands is often this: "You're the problem." That kind of message hurts. It leaves your partner feeling rejected, blamed, or shut out. And in that pain, their Protector steps in. You both shift into your self-protective moves. Likely, one lashes out, the other retreats or shuts down.

Problem 3: We Assume Our Intention is Obvious

Most people assume their partner knows what they mean or automatically understands the intention behind their words. Yet, as the listener, you tend to hear what you fear.

If there's any doubt or ambiguity, your nervous system won't default to a generous interpretation. It will scan for the worst-case scenario to stay safe. It's not personal, it's biology.

For example, you might ask, "Are you going to clean the kitchen today?" thinking you're simply checking on a shared task. But your partner might hear this as a criticism or a passive-aggressive jab, even if that wasn't your intention.

Problem 4: Our Emotions Leak Sideways

Unspoken emotions are another common source of miscommunication. When we don't acknowledge or express our feelings, those emotions don't just disappear. They tend to leak out in our tone, body language, or choice of words, often without us even realizing it.

Imagine coming home after a long, stressful day. You're worn out and overstimulated. Your partner asks, "What do you want to do for dinner?" and you reply, "I don't care, do whatever you want."

You think you're being easygoing. But if your voice telgraphs the weight of your stress, your partner might hear frustration, resentment, or distance. Your intention is to be agreeable, but the impact is rejection. Without naming what's going on underneath, "I'm fried, and I just need a moment to breathe," your words can easily be misinterpreted.

See the Dance

When communication breaks down, it often feels like two people talking *at* each other, not *with* each other. This is the "vicious cycle."

Take Jordan and Morgan as an example. Jordan has been logging long hours at work. Morgan has been feeling increasingly lonely.

Morgan says: "We never spend time together anymore."

- ▸ **Intention:** "I miss you. I feel lonely. I want to feel like I matter to you."
- ▸ **Impact (What Jordan hears):** "You are failing me. You are a bad partner."

Jordan responds: "I'm working hard for us! That's not true, I'm here, aren't I?"

- ▸ **Intention:** "I feel unappreciated and stressed. I need you to see how hard I'm trying."
- ▸ **Impact (What Morgan hears):** "My feelings are wrong. My needs don't matter."

This is a classic miscommunication. Two people talking. Clear about their intentions, but unaware of their impact. Both retreat into their protective responses, complaining and defending, and the distance between them grows.

The next step is developing awareness of your relational dance, the back-and-forth patterns that shape how you interact. This idea comes from Dr. Sue Johnson and her work in Emotionally Focused Therapy (EFT). In EFT, couples are invited to recognize the dance of conflict, not each other, as the problem.

Imagine standing shoulder to shoulder with your partner, looking at your relationship from the outside. You're not in the dance anymore. You're observing it. That distance gives you objectivity and compassion. You're not the enemy, and neither is your partner. The dance is the problem.

Let's look at how this might play out if Jordan and Morgan take that outside-in perspective:

Morgan starts: "I was feeling disconnected, but instead of telling you that, I said something that felt safer, 'We never spend time together anymore.' I think it probably came across as criticism."

Jordan reflects: "I heard that and felt accused, like I'm failing you. So, I got defensive. Instead of hearing that you miss me, I said, 'That's not true, I'm here, aren't I?'"

Morgan nods: "Right, and when that didn't land how I hoped, I felt even more hurt. So I pushed again, 'You're always on your phone.'"

Jordan responds: "And I doubled down. I felt judged and said, 'I'm working hard for us.' I was trying to explain, but really, I was protecting myself."

Now that they've named the pattern, they take the sting out of it. Instead of thinking, *Why do they always do this?* they can step back and say, *Ah, we're doing that thing again, the criticism-defensiveness dance.*

It's not personal. It's a pattern. Once they can see it clearly, they can start changing their dance steps, together.

Slowing Down

The good news is that these patterns can shift, often with one small, powerful change: slowing down. Reacting on autopilot keeps us stuck. But a pause? A pause gives you just enough room to choose differently.

Slowing down gives your nervous system a moment to catch up. It creates space to clarify your thoughts, check in with your body, and find the words that reflect your heart.

Effective Internal Action

You can't stop emotions from happening. But you *can* change how you respond to them. When a strong emotion hits, try this:

1. **Notice the physical response.** Tightness? Heat? Shaky hands? Your body is sending signals.

   My chest tightened, my jaw clenched, and heat rose to my face as I stared at the unread messages on my phone. The longer I waited, the worse it felt.

2. **Name the core emotion.** Naming it reduces its power. For example, "I feel angry" or "I feel scared."

   I wanted to say I was just frustrated, but when I took a deep breath and sat with it, I realized underneath the frustration, I felt hurt.

3. **Identify the story.**

   My mind jumped in: *If they cared, they wouldn't ignore me.* The same story I had told myself before. The one that made every unanswered message feel like proof that I wasn't important.

4. **Challenge the story.** Is it true? Or is it just a well-worn script from the past?

   Was it true? Could something else be going on? Maybe they were caught up in work, lost in thought, or assuming we'd talk later. Perhaps this wasn't about me at all.

That slight pause can change things. Instead of sending a passive-aggressive message, you can reach out with curiosity instead of assumption:

"Hey, I noticed I haven't heard from you today. Is everything okay?"

And just like that, you shift from reacting emotionally to responding intentionally, which makes all the difference.

Outsmarting the Nervous System

Before you can show up as your Connected Self in your relationship, you have to understand how your own nervous system responds to stress. Each of us develops automatic patterns that kick in when we sense danger, often without realizing it. Sometimes these patterns make perfect sense based on past experiences, but they can also keep us stuck in reactive loops.

Here is a simple example from my own life that shows how the nervous system can create and reinforce these patterns, and how awareness can help you change them.

When my son was young, he would sometimes experience sudden spells of anxiety. Out of nowhere, his heart would race and his stomach would ache. At first, these episodes seemed random, just physical sensations that came and went. But over time, his nervous system began to link a racing heart with anxiety itself. Soon, his racing heart triggered more anxiety and his nervous system doubled down on its response. Anxiety would bring the racing heart, the racing heart would reinforce the anxiety, and the cycle would spiral.

What started as a symptom became a trigger. A feedback loop developed:

- ▶ His heart would race.
- ▶ His body interpreted this as a sign of danger.
- ▶ His anxiety increased.
- ▶ The cycle repeated.

This pattern makes perfect sense when you consider how the nervous system works. It prioritizes efficiency over precision. If something felt threatening in the past, it doesn't stop to ask, "Is this dangerous now?" It just reacts.

But here's the good news. The nervous system is adaptable. Just as it can create unhelpful patterns, it can also unlearn them.

My son was able to outsmart this feedback loop over time with self-soothing strategies and growing self-awareness. He learned to pause, recognize the signals his body was sending, and use tools to calm his nervous system. That is how he broke the cycle and began to reclaim control.

With self-awareness and the right tools, you can rewire your responses.

Calming the System

Once my son understood that his racing heart wasn't the enemy, we worked on ways to calm his nervous system. These same strategies apply to anyone wanting to shift out of reactivity and into presence.

Breathing Techniques

Breathing is the fastest way to signal safety to your nervous system. This breathing technique became my son's go-to:

- ▶ Inhale a deep breath, mouth closed, through your nose.
- ▶ When you think you've inhaled deeply, inhale again.
- ▶ Hold your breath for 10 counts.
- ▶ Exhale slowly through your mouth for 10 counts or until your breath is released.

Slowing the exhale activates the parasympathetic nervous system, the part of your body responsible for rest and calm. Over time, this breathing technique rewires your system to default to regulation instead of panic.

Reframing the Sensation

Instead of fearing his racing heart, my son learned to change the story around it: "A racing heart doesn't mean I'm in danger. It's just my body's natural response." Reframing changes the story you tell yourself. Mantras also offer a comforting anchor: "I am safe. This will pass."

This simple shift in perception disrupted the cycle. Instead of reinforcing anxiety, it helped my son step outside of it. When your body gets stuck in the past, grounding pulls you back into the present.

The 5-4-3-2-1 Method:

▶ Name **five** things you can see.

▶ Name **four** things you can touch.

▶ Name **three** things you can hear.

▶ Name **two** things you can smell.

▶ Name **one** thing you can taste.

This practice gives your mind a different focus, helping you step out of reactive loops and into the now.

Movement to Reset

Sometimes, moving your body is the best way to break an emotional cycle.

▶ Shake your hands.

▶ Jump up and down.

▶ Stretch.

▶ Take a walk.

Movement burns off excess adrenaline, creating space for your system to reset.

Mantras and Reassurance

Words matter. The way you talk to yourself in instances of reactivity can either escalate or defuse the situation.

Two simple mantras we used:

▶ "This is just my body reacting. It will pass."

▶ "I've been here before and know how to calm myself."

Repeating these phrases interrupts the fear cycle and reminds your system that you are in control.

The Power of Practice

At first, these tools might feel like extra steps, something you must remember to do in the heat of the moment. But over time, with repetition, they become second nature.

At an early age, my son learned to spot the warning signs before anxiety spiraled. Instead of reacting automatically, he'd pause:

"Okay, I know what to do."

And the more he practiced, the more his nervous system adapted.

Instead of reinforcing the old loop (racing heart = panic), his body started learning a new association: *A racing heart isn't dangerous. I can calm it.*

The same is true for you.

Whenever you choose awareness over reaction, you teach your nervous system something new.

Relational Effective Action

In intimate relationships, your self-protective instincts show up faster and louder than anywhere else. Once you understand what is happening inside your body and have tools to calm your system, the next step is deciding how you want to show up with your partner. This is where you move from automatic reactions to intentional responses.

Leveling Up: Choosing an Opposite Action

One powerful way to do this comes from Dialectical Behavior Therapy (DBT), developed by Dr. Marsha Linehan. DBT is a therapeutic approach that helps manage intense emotions and build healthier communication skills. A useful tool for intimate relationships is what she calls Opposite Action.

Opposite action is the conscious decision to choose behaviors that run counter to your defensive instincts. Instead of letting your nervous system drive the car, you pause and use your urge to self-protect as a cue to shift toward intentional, mindful, connected communication. The goal isn't to ignore your instincts; it's to honor them as signals while still choosing the behavior that supports connection.

For instance, if you are overwhelmed and feel the urge to withdraw, the opposite action encourages you to stay engaged, even if only for a short moment longer. If you are inclined to escalate the situation by raising your voice, the opposite action suggests slowing your pace, lowering your voice, and softening your body to de-escalate the conflict.

Rather than trying to eliminate defensive behaviors, opposite action helps you use them as information. The urge itself becomes your reminder: I am activated. This is my chance to choose connection instead of protection. This space is where change happens. It is where you move from reacting to relating, and from protecting yourself to building connection. A list of Opposite Actions is available in the Appendix.

Leveling Up in Action

Let's see how this plays out with a real couple.

Marley and Indigo are discussing weekend plans. Lately, Marley has felt left out because Indigo often makes plans without checking in first. As the conversation unfolds, Marley's heart starts to race. That familiar urge to lash out rises, and the words come out sharp, accusing Indigo of being inconsiderate.

Indigo, caught off guard and feeling attacked, raises their voice in defense.

Now both Marley and Indigo feel emotionally activated. The conversation teeters on the edge of disconnection. But this is also an opportunity for something different.

Instead of reacting, Marley notices what is happening inside. The heat in the chest. The tightness in the throat. The old, familiar narrative starting to play. Rather than follow that urge, Marley takes a breath and leans into vulnerability.

"When you work late," Marley says, "I feel hurt. And the story I make up is that you do not enjoy being with me as much as I enjoy being with you."

This is the shift that changes everything.

Indigo is invited into Marley's experience, and the urge to defend softens. When a partner's Protector steps back, connection becomes possible. Compassion starts to rise naturally, almost instinctively.

This is what it means to choose an opposite action.

Personal Reflection and Commitment

Consider your own patterns. When you feel hurt or triggered in a conversation, what do you usually do? Do you raise your voice? Shut down? Get sarcastic? Try to fix things quickly so the discomfort goes away?

Now ask yourself this: What might an opposite behavior look like for you? What would it sound like to slow down, to name what you are feeling, or to stay curious instead of shutting the conversation down? These small shifts are powerful, and they are entirely within reach.

Reflection Exercise
1. Identify Your Top 3 Defenses

▸ The damaging defense I use most often is: _____.

▸ Another one I recognize in myself is: _____.

▸ A third that impacts my relationships is: _____.

2. Pick One to Shift This Week

Which opposite action will you practice the next time you notice defensiveness?

▶ Instead of _____, I will try _____.

3. Practice a Repair Statement

If you slip into an old pattern, how will you repair it?

▶ "I realize I just _____ (damaging defense).

▶ I am working on _____ (opposite action).

▶ Can we try again?"

For a complete list of common defensive patterns and their opposite actions, see the Appendix on page 227. It is a helpful way to identify your own protective instincts and begin practicing new ones.

As you start to notice your Protector and practice the pause, you will also start to notice something else. Intense feelings come with a pull, a push, a strong inner pressure to do something. To walk away. To shut down. To argue. To fix. To please. These urges are the nervous system's first draft of a plan for how to protect you. Opposite action gives you a way to pause, feel that pull, and then choose a response that actually supports the relationship you want to build.

Step 1: Pause and Choose a Better Action

The next time you feel yourself getting activated, try asking:

▶ What am I really feeling right now? (e.g., "I feel lonely.")
▶ What do I want my partner to understand? (e.g., "I want them to know I miss them.")
▶ How can I say this in a way that invites *connection* instead of *conflict*?

Take Avery and Ash. Avery says, "Do you really need to spend all weekend on that project?"

- ▶ **Intention:** "I want to spend time together."
- ▶ **Impact:** Ash hears criticism and responds defensively: "It's not like this is for fun!"

Imagine if Avery had paused and expressed the *intention* clearly: "I've been feeling disconnected and was hoping we could spend some time together this weekend. Is there a way to make that happen?"

By naming feelings and inviting participation, Avery could have avoided triggering defensiveness and invited Ash to care.

Step 2: Check In and Repair (When You Get It Wrong)

You will get it wrong. Your words won't land as intended. When that happens, the goal is to repair.

Checking in with your partner is one of the most direct ways to confirm that your words are landing as intended. Instead of assuming your message was understood, ask.

- ▶ **For the Speaker:** "Hey, based on your response, I don't think you heard that the way I meant it. Let me try again." Or, "What are you hearing me say?"

- ▶ **For the Listener:** It's easy to get stuck in our interpretation, hearing what we fear. Instead of reacting impulsively, we can say, "Here's what I heard. Did I get it?"

This lets your partner explain or reframe their message: "That's not what I meant. Let me try again."

When miscommunication happens, own it. Saying something like, "I think that came out wrong. What I meant to say is..." demonstrates a willingness to reconnect. The aim is to create understanding, not to get everything right.

Step 3: Handle Hard Conversations with Thoughtfulness

Some of the most important conversations are also the hardest. Maybe you need to set a boundary or address a behavior causing tension.

Effective communication doesn't mean avoiding these topics; it means approaching them thoughtfully.

- ▶ **Story Blaming:** "You never listen to me." (You get into story, act as if it's true, and use it to blame your partner).

- ▶ **Constructive Sharing:** "I've been feeling unheard, and I'd appreciate it if we could slow down and listen to each other more during conversations." (This invites collaboration.)

Timing also plays a crucial role, as we'll explore in the next section, Wholehearted Communication. Even the most carefully chosen words can backfire if the timing isn't right. Bringing up a loaded topic when you're both calm and present creates the conditions for a productive, connective conversation.

This Will Feel Awkward (And That's Okay)

As you continue reading, you'll soon be introduced to scripted conversations designed to help you communicate more effectively. Now's a good time to remind you that this rarely feels natural at first.

A common reaction in my classes is when couples use these scripts for the first time and laugh, cringe, or look at each other skeptically. I often hear partners say, "This feels awkward," or "We would never talk like this."

That clunky, vulnerable feeling is totally normal. And honestly, it's also when most people are tempted to quit.

Don't. The scripts are a tool to help you slow down, connect, and stay grounded. They give your nervous system something to hold onto while you build new habits. And if we're being real here, these conversations could save you a whole lot of time, frustration, and even money.

Ask yourself: What's the alternative? More arguments? More silence? More sessions in therapy? A breakup?

You don't have to get it all right. You won't. The goal is progress, to move toward connection. And right now, we're aiming for effective, not effortless.

Practice Makes Progress

Couples who are successful with Wholehearted Communication often start by spending up to ninety minutes on a single topic. It can feel painful for both partners. This is a relationship workout. Even when couples follow the structure, their early instinct is to focus on facts and stories instead of feelings.

After five conversations, couples begin to see the value of the approach. After ten, there's often a sense of hope. By twenty, many start to wonder how they managed without these guardrails.

A year into using Wholehearted Communication consistently, the payoff is clear: fewer blowups, a greater sense of steadiness, and more confidence that when conflict shows up (not if), the tools to address it are already in place.

By the second year of practice, it's common for committed couples to find that even their most challenging topics rarely take more than thirty minutes. And when the conversation ends, it ends. They don't carry the residue into the rest of the day or week.

That's the real payoff. Not just shorter conversations, but cleaner ones. Conversations that resolve instead of linger.

This work is an investment. What you put in early, even when it feels slow or uncomfortable, pays off in clarity, connection, and peace over time.

III.

THE ART OF
WHOLEHEARTED
COMMUNICATION

"Do you want
to be helped,
heard, or hugged?"

— JANCEE DUNN, *The New York Times*

CHAPTER 10

Types of Conversations

Have you ever stopped to consider how many different kinds of conversations you have in a single day?

Sometimes, you chat, sharing little moments, joking around, or discussing what's for dinner. Other times, you're reminiscing about that one trip where everything went sideways (and you still laugh about it). You might find yourself telling a story from your day, hoping your partner hears you, not just the words, but *you*.

Then there are those conversations where you're trying to figure something out together, make a decision, solve a problem, or plan what's next. And let's be honest, sometimes you're just trying not to lose your cool when things get tense, when a value clash shows up, or you're knee-deep in a misunderstanding.

Not All Conversations are the Same

Knowing what kind of conversation you are having is a helpful start to good communication. Let's explore the five types of conversations.

1. Everyday Conversations

Everyday Conversations are those easy, ordinary interactions, the small moments that hold your relationship together. Relationship researcher John Gottman emphasizes the importance of these interactions through what he calls "bids for connection," when one partner reaches out, seeking attention, affection, or simply a bit of understanding.

These bids might seem minor, a comment about your day, a quick text message, or even a casual glance, but they're powerful opportunities to build intimacy and trust. Recognizing and responding positively to these bids creates a sense of closeness that strengthens your emotional bond.

According to Gottman, couples who consistently make and positively respond to these bids tend to have stronger, more resilient relationships.

2. Personal Sharing

When we first fall in love, we experience an enormous learning curve as we get to know and understand our partner. To learn about each other, we engage in conversations that involve Personal Sharing, such as stories about your past, your quirks and idiosyncrasies, and discussions of your fears, hurts, successes, and dreams. Anything that reveals who you are counts as personal sharing, and where true intimacy begins.

Personal Sharing invites vulnerability and opening up your inner world, thoughts, feelings, experiences, and aspirations and inviting your partner to step into it. These deeper conversations go beyond surface-level exchanges to create a space where you can see each other. This is different from reporting the details of your day or debating the latest news. When your partner meets you in that space with curiosity and compassion, a bridge of trust is built that strengthens your bond.

Real intimacy grows when both partners feel seen and understood. When your partner opens up, respond with sincerity and curiosity, setting aside distractions to give them your full attention.

Unilateral Downloading

One of the easy traps to fall into with Personal Sharing is what I call unilateral downloading. That's when one partner talks and talks, maybe unloading about work, family, or the latest drama, without leaving much space for the other. It can feel like sharing, but it's really more like delivering a monologue.

This type of one-sided communication where one partner unloads their thoughts, feelings, or frustrations *at* their partner, rather than *with* them, creates a one-way street. One person is transmitting, and the other is expected to just receive. This does not create intimacy. It actually creates distance.

Personal Sharing isn't about reporting every detail of your day or downloading your inner world without pause. It's about opening a door and saying, "Come in, I want you to see this part of me." When you download without dialogue, your partner can start to feel less like a teammate and more like a captive audience. True intimacy grows when you slow down, invite curiosity, and make room for both voices.

3. Decision-Making Conversations

While Everyday Conversations focus on maintaining connection and Personal Sharing fosters intimacy through vulnerability, Decision-Making Conversations serve a different purpose: collaboration and mutual understanding. These conversations are less about emotional depth and more about making practical choices. Some decisions are small but mighty, like "What do you want for dinner?" (I mean, are you even in a relationship if you haven't had this conversation?) Others, however, carry much more weight and have far more impactful consequences.

Most people value compromise, splitting the difference, or taking turns so no one feels they've "lost" when making decisions. However, I'm not a fan of compromise for big relationship decisions. Instead, Wholehearted Communication relies on Relationship-Affirming Decisions.

I discovered the pitfalls of compromise a few decades ago in one of my first serious relationships. We both started out living in the same city until I received a job offer in a town an hour away. Thinking we were being fair, we moved halfway between her workplace and mine. On paper, it seemed logical, yet in reality, we landed in a small town with limited diversity and little connection to our social networks. By trying to appease both sides, we ended up with a solution that didn't serve our relationship.

A Relationship-Affirming Decision involves both partners considering each option's impact on their well-being, needs, and relationship. When making Relationship-Affirming Decisions, the question becomes: "How does this add to our relationship?" It is also important to consider: "How does this decision detract from our relationship?"

When you commit to sharing your life with someone, your life transitions from "me" to "we." Every decision you make will affect your partner and vice versa. There's a saying I once heard that I've found to be true in relationships: "A bad decision made together is better than a good decision made alone."

Every choice you make, individually and as a couple, will either add to or take away from your connection. Making a Relationship-Affirming Decision involves some math: you factor in all the positive impacts of your decision, then subtract the negative impact, and identify the path with the most positive total impact. By focusing on the "we," you increase the odds that both partners stay aligned with what really matters.

4. Requesting Advice

Giving and receiving advice might seem straightforward, but it's one of the trickiest conversations in a relationship. Why? Because advice, when mishandled, can feel dismissive, controlling, or even invalidating, especially when it's not invited. When you ask for advice, it can feel vulnerable. It's saying, "I'm unsure, and I need help." How you respond to a request for advice matters just as much as when you're the one seeking guidance.

Here's a real-life example. One evening, Skylar came home feeling overwhelmed about a work situation. "I don't know what to do about this project," Skylar said. Before Skylar finished speaking, Emerson jumped in: "Here's what you should do. Start by talking to your manager, and then . . ."

Skylar went silent and nodded politely but later shared, "I didn't need you to fix it. I just needed you to listen."

No matter how well-intentioned, offering unsolicited advice can come across as dismissive. It can feel like you're saying, "I know you better than you know yourself."

Advice must support, not control, your partner. Even well-meaning suggestions can land as criticism or control, especially if they're unsolicited. That's why the best starting point is curiosity. A simple question like, "Would you like my advice on this, or do you just need me to listen?" can change the entire tone of the conversation. It shows respect for your partner's autonomy and acknowledges that you're there to meet them where they are, not to impose your solutions.

A simple way to do this is by using the "Three H's." When your partner comes to you with a problem, pause and ask: "Do you want to be Helped, Heard, or Hugged?"

- **Helped:** They want your perspective, a brainstorm, or a solution.
- **Heard:** They just need to vent and feel understood without being fixed.
- **Hugged:** They are overstimulated or hurting and just need physical or emotional comfort.

By identifying the "H" before you respond, you ensure your impact matches your intention.

When advice is given or received with respect, it becomes a loving act of care. It shows that your partner's struggles matter to you, that you're invested in their growth, and that you're willing to share your experience to help them. But if advice is rushed, unsolicited, or controlling, it can unintentionally create distance, leaving one partner feeling dismissed or the other feeling unheard.

Emerson and Skylar eventually found their balance. When Skylar comes home with a dilemma, Emerson pauses before jumping in. "What do you need from me right now?" Emerson asks. Sometimes, Skylar just needs to vent. Other times, Skylar says, "I'd love your thoughts." And when that happens, Emerson offers advice without expecting Skylar to agree.

Advice is more than problem-solving; it's about showing up for your partner in a way that strengthens trust and connection. So, pause the next time your partner comes to you for help. Advice is best received when it's invited. And it's best given from a place of respect, curiosity, and understanding.

5. Wholehearted Communication

We've already talked about the first four types of conversations: the Everyday check-ins, the Personal Sharing, the collaborative Decision-Making, and the requests for Advice. These are all crucial. They keep life moving and help us feel connected day-to-day.

But then there are the conversations that feel different.

The ones where something's off. Where there's tension in the room, a comment that landed sideways, or a need that isn't being met. The ones where your nervous system perks up and your usual tools don't seem to be working.

That's where Wholehearted Communication comes in.

Wholehearted conversations aren't just about talking things through. They're about showing up, really showing up, with curiosity, courage, and care. They're about staying in the room when your instincts tell you to shut down or push back. They're about softening, not hardening, and leaning in, not out.

This kind of communication doesn't come from being right. It comes from being willing. Willing to slow down. Willing to notice your patterns.

Willing to choose connection over control. To say, "This matters and so do we."

In the pages ahead, we will explore what these conversations look like, how to tell what kind of conversation you're in, and what to do when the heat rises. Because I think we can all agree that those more difficult interactions will happen, the question is, how will you show up when they do?

Recognizing the Levels of Conflict: Smoke, Fire, and Wildfire

When something feels off in a relationship, do you pause and say, "Huh, I wonder what's really going on here?" If you're like most people, probably not. It's more likely that you react. You shut down, get defensive, change the subject, or come in swinging. It's not because you're bad at communication. It's because you are human. And, as we've established earlier, your nervous system is wired to protect you.

Wholehearted Communication invites a different path. Instead of letting those first signs of tension run the show, it's a signal to take a breath. Just one breath. That pause may feel small, but it creates a space to shift from self-protection to connection. This isn't about pretending everything's fine when it's not. It's about learning to show up with an *effective* approach. In Wholehearted Communication, conflict is divided into three levels: *Smoke, Fire,* and *Wildfire.*

Level 1: Smoke

This is mostly what couples deal with in their day-to-day lives. These are the early signs of disconnection. A sharp tone. A missed bid for attention. A sigh that says more than words. It's not a full-blown conflict yet, but something's stirring.

Level 2: Fire

Now imagine the same dynamic, but this time, the tension's been simmering for a while. Maybe it's been weeks of rushed dinners, missed goodnight kisses, and that heavy, hollow feeling of two people sharing space but not connection. Ships passing in the night.

So, when the complaint about the dishes finally lands, it hits differently. It is no longer about the dishes. It's about something much deeper.

Instead of softening or leaning in, you might snap: "Why is it always about what I didn't do?" And your partner fires back:

"Because I feel like I'm the only one trying around here!"

The temperature rises. You both retreat to your corners, carrying not just the frustration of this interaction but also the weight of everything left unsaid. If the smoke is ignored long enough, the flames become visible. And if you're not careful, those flames will spread.

What separates Level 2 from Level 1 is both the intensity of the conflict and the meaning behind it.

When we feel lonely or unseen, it's easy to fixate on what's in front of us: the dirty dishes, the laundry pile, the forgotten text. But those aren't the real issues. They're just the flare-ups. What's really hurting is the deeper emotional wound underneath.

Most of the time, those wounds aren't even about our partner; they're shaped by the stories we carry from long ago. Stories about our worth. Our lovability. Whether or not we belong.

So instead of snapping back, what if you said:

"When you get frustrated about the dishes, I feel unseen, and I make up the story that you do not see everything I do around here, only what I don't do. I would love for us to feel like a team again."

Yes, that kind of vulnerability can feel like stepping right into the fire.

And, ironically enough, it's also the very thing that helps put it out.

Wholehearted Communication teaches us how to handle Level 2 issues by narrowing the focus, not spiraling into every past frustration or pointing fingers, but slowing down, getting curious, and naming what's happening underneath and within.

It takes practice. And we'll get into the "how" soon. For now, what matters most is recognizing when the smoke has turned to fire and being willing to try something different.

Level 3: Wildfire

If fire is hard to put out, wildfire is what happens when the flames catch the wind. This is when one conflict bleeds into another: last week's money fight resurfaces, that forgotten anniversary from five years ago makes a cameo. Suddenly, the conversation about dishes turns into a discussion about *everything*. The tone shifts. The stakes feel higher. And the foundation of your relationship starts to feel shaky.

At this point, it's no longer about the issue in front of you. It's about all the hurts that haven't been healed, all the words left unsaid, all the negative patterns that have worn grooves into your connection. It's where blame takes center stage, defensiveness runs the show, and exhaustion sets in like a heavy fog. Nothing feels safe. Nothing feels fixable.

The good news? Even wildfires can be contained.

Firefighters don't try to douse every flame at once. They work strategically. They clear a path. They protect what matters most. They focus on where the fire is hottest. And that's precisely what Wholehearted Communication invites you to do.

You're not fighting *each other;* you're fighting the fire. Together.

LEVEL SYSTEM

SMOKE
LEVEL 1

- Noticable shifts in tone and body language
- Minor, disconnects – in the moment
- Prevent misunderstandings from escalating
- Early warning signs that can be quickly addressed

FIRE
LEVEL 2

- Obvious tension and strong emotions
- Frequent or prolonged misunderstandings
- Escalating conflicts requiring intervention

WILDFIRE
LEVEL 3

- Open, intense conflict
- Urgent, crisis-level issues
- Emotional chaos

A Path Out of the Fire

At Level 3, when the wildfire is raging, the only way forward is together. This is where your nervous system is fully activated, your heart is pounding, and everything in you wants to protect, defend, or retreat.

But just like firefighters have tools, so do you. You have:

▸ Your wise mind.

▸ Shared values and a history worth protecting.

▸ And most importantly, each other.

You don't have to fix everything in one conversation. That's not the goal. The goal is to slow the fire down. To create enough emotional safety that you can both step out of the flames and reconnect. Because when you shift from *me* versus *you* to *us* versus *the fire*, that's where the healing begins.

The beauty of Wholehearted Communication lies in its practicality. It's not just a philosophy; it's a tangible set of tools, frameworks, and scripts designed to meet you where you are and guide you toward where you want to be.

In the chapters ahead, you'll discover how to navigate conversations at any level, whether it's a tiny flicker of tension, a flare-up of emotion, or a full-blown wildfire. You'll get a framework that's not just effective, but also dependable. And if you commit to using it as it's designed, it works.

Wholehearted Communication is more than a tool for talking; it's a reliable pathway to getting back to each other. It helps you move through conflict without losing connection. It gives you language when words are hard to find. And maybe most importantly, it offers a way to repair what's been hurt and build something stronger in its place.

No matter how far apart you feel, there is a path back. This is how you find it together.

"Perhaps everything that frightens us is, in its deepest essence, something helpless that wants our love."

— RAINER MARIA RILKE

CHAPTER 11

Scale of Distress

Have you ever had a super-sized reaction to something that, later, seemed ...kind of minor?

You and your partner are on your way to meet your parents for dinner. As you enter a parking spot, your partner gestures toward it and says, "There's a spot." You shoot back sarcastically, with a harsh tone, "Thank you, Dr. Obvious!"

You're both parked a minute later, voices raised, saying things that feel sharp and maybe even a little mean. You're sitting in silence, wondering how it all unraveled so fast.

Looking back, you realize this wasn't really about the parking spot. It was never about the parking spot. It was about two people already on edge because, let's face it, meeting your parents is stressful. Because you were both holding unspoken tension. That comment, harmless on the surface, landed in a body that was already bracing for something challenging.

The Scale of Distress

In the parking lot example, the stimulus was low. Your partner simply pointed out a spot you were already pulling into. But the response? A sarcastic, high-volume snap.

That mismatch is the key. It's a clue that there's something more going on beneath the surface.

This is where the Scale of Distress comes in. The goal is not to label your behavior as "good" or "bad." The Scale of Distress is designed for *noticing*. It helps you pause and ask, "Does my reaction fit this situation?"

When anger, anxiety, or hurt spikes over something relatively minor, it often signals nervous system activation. Past experiences and unresolved emotions can attach themselves to present-day situations, prompting your body to react as if there's danger when there isn't.

The Scale of Distress helps you catch that activation in real time. And when you can catch it, you have options. You can pause. You can regulate. You can choose connection instead of escalation.

Over time, increased awareness leads to more intentional responses. Those responses are what build emotional safety in a relationship.

Understanding the Scale of Distress

The Scale of Distress is divided into three ranges:

- ▸ Safe (0–3)
- ▸ Moderate (4–6)
- ▸ High (7–10)

Each range offers insights into your emotional state and indicates how to respond constructively.

Safe Range (0–3): Gratitude and Collaboration

In the safe range, emotions are manageable, and you feel grounded. This is the space for gratitude, calm communication, and collaboration. Addressing concerns in this range allows you to resolve minor issues before they escalate.

Signs you're in the safe range:

- ▸ You feel a slight unease or frustration, but it doesn't cloud your clarity.
- ▸ You are open to communication without getting defensive.
- ▸ You feel a sense of connection and willingness to work together.

Example: Your partner forgets to pick up an item from the store. While slightly frustrating, it's clear they didn't intend harm. You address it calmly:

> "Hey, when I heard you forgot to pick up milk, I felt stressed about dinner, and the story I make up is that what's important to me isn't important to you."

(This approach uses a tool we'll explore in depth later, the No-Fault Formula. For now, just notice how it keeps the interaction constructive and focused on teamwork.)

Moderate Range (4–6): Regulation and Grounding

In this range, emotions are heightened but still within your control. This is the "Fire" level (Level 2). This range is pivotal. If left unchecked, emotions will likely escalate into defensiveness, withdrawal, or conflict.

Signs you're in the moderate range:

- ▶ Physical cues like a racing heartbeat or tight shoulders.
- ▶ Urges to interrupt, defend, or emotionally withdraw.
- ▶ Struggling to stay present while still trying to engage.

Reactions in this range suggest that there is resonance between what is happening now and what happened in the past. For instance, a comment from your partner may feel disproportionately critical if it reminds you of times when you felt judged.

For example, your partner makes a comment about how you handled a situation with a friend. Defensiveness rises. Instead of reacting impulsively, you pause, ground yourself, and respond:

> "When you said that, I felt defensive because I make up the story that you think I didn't handle it well. Can we slow down and talk this through?"

Regulation Tools (for Moderate Activation)

When you feel yourself entering this range, your first job is to calm your nervous system.

▶ **Deep Breathing:** Breathe in slowly through your nose for a count of four. Hold that breath for a count of four. Then exhale gently through your mouth for a count of six. This intentional breathing helps settle your nervous system.

▶ **Grounding Through Sensation**: Bring your attention to your body. Feel your feet on the floor. Notice the support of the chair beneath you. Pay attention to the sensation of your hands resting in your lap. This physical awareness pulls you out of your spinning thoughts and back into the present moment.

High Range (7–10): Safety and Self-Care

This is the "Wildfire" range (Level 3). It reflects emotional overwhelm, or what Dr. John Gottman calls "flooding." In this state, your nervous system triggers fight, flight, freeze, fix, fawn or flop responses. Your logical brain goes 'offline,' making it biologically impossible to think clearly or engage constructively.

Signs you're in the high range:

▶ Intense urges to yell, shut down, or walk away.

▶ Spiraling thoughts of worst-case scenarios.

▶ Physical distress, such as a racing heart or clenched fists.

High emotional states often reveal old wounds. The intensity of your reaction is almost certainly tied to past experiences. For example, your partner criticizes your spending, and your anger flares. Instead of snapping, pause, and ask for a break:

"I'm feeling overwhelmed and don't think I can talk about this calmly right now. Can we take a break and revisit it later?"

Level 10: Crisis

A Level 10 is not a relationship problem. It is a safety emergency.

At this level, distress has moved beyond flooding into immediate danger, whether that means you are at risk of harming yourself, your partner is, or the situation has escalated to physical violence. This is not the time for communication strategies or a cooling-off walk. This is the time to call 911.

No framework, script, or breathing exercise applies here. Get safe first. Everything else comes later.

Self-Regulation Tools (for High Activation)

When you are this activated, simple breathing might not be enough. Your body needs to release that energy.

▸ **Movement:** Physical movement can help release the flood of stress hormones. Take a walk (separately), stretch your arms and legs, or shake out your hands. This signals to your nervous system that you are not in danger.

▸ **Soothing Self-Talk:** You might say, "It's okay to feel this. I am noticing the sensations in my body, and I will allow them to move through me." This creates internal safety and reminds you that emotions are messengers, not emergencies.

SITUATION	DISTRESS RATING
Safety, trust, caring, playfulness, affection	**0** COMFORTABLE — *Relaxed. Happy. Content.*
Hunger, fatigue, mild stress, physical unease	**1** UNCOMFORTABLE — *Discomfort.*
Trivial disagreements, small forgetfulness	**2** DISPLEASED — *Uneasy. Tense.*
Inattentive comments, minor neglect in tasks	**3** UNSURE — *Unhappy. Mild Hurt.*
Dismissive, preoccupied, inadvertent rudeness, excessive teasing	**4** FRUSTRATED — *Hurt. Agitated.*
Misaligned expectations, habitual tardiness, recurring #2-4	**5** DISAPPOINTED — *Anxious. Concerned. Unsure.*
Unreliability, mixed messages, differing values, feelings, and needs	**6** UPSET — *Confused. Uncertain. Angry.*
Criticism, defensiveness, blaming, mild threats, emotional withdrawal	**7** HURT — *Alone. Inadequate. Defeated.*
Boundary violations, deception, stonewalling, contempt, recurring #5-7	**8** DISTRESSED — *Rejected. Emotionally Unsafe.*
Dishonest actions, infidelity, trust breaches	**9** TRAUMATIZED — *Powerless. Overwhelmed. Hurt.*
When you are physically unsafe, talking will not help - CALL 911	**10** PANIC/TERROR — *Powerless. Physically Unsafe.*

LEVEL 1 · LEVEL 2 · LEVEL 3 · 911

lesbian**love**adv.com

The 24-Hour Rule: The Commitment to Repair

Taking a break isn't stonewalling or dropping out of the conversation. It's a strategic pause to prepare yourself to handle the issue well.

However, this pause comes with a disclaimer: You must commit to returning to the conversation within twenty-four hours. This allows you to address what happened thoughtfully, after both of your nervous systems are calm.

Putting the Scale to Work

Keeping a visual reminder of the Scale of Distress on your phone or in a notebook can help you check in with yourself before reacting.

With this tool, you gain awareness. With awareness, you can pause. And in that pause, you can choose a more constructive response that supports emotional safety and nurtures the connection in your relationship.

Recognizing Patterns of Escalation and Triggers

The Scale of Distress is designed to help you identify your patterns of escalation. A forgotten task, a casual comment, or a missed bid for connection can suddenly trigger intense emotional responses. These heightened reactions often indicate unresolved pain that intensifies your feelings.

Reflection Questions:

▶ When have I felt this way before?

▶ What past hurt or unmet need most closely resembles this?

▶ How can I respond in a way that reflects the present rather than the past?

When you notice tension rising or after a difficult moment has passed, pause to check in with yourself. Where are you on the Scale right now? What might help you regulate before moving forward? You can use these questions in real time to slow down a reaction or afterward to understand what was happening inside you. Either way, naming your emotional state begins to shift it. Each time you pause to notice, you strengthen your ability to choose connection over reaction, and that is what builds real strength in a relationship.

"He gains much who knows how to seize the right moment."

- HORACE

CHAPTER 12

The Pre-Conversation Setup

Timing, Consent, and Readiness

It's instinctive to believe that serious conversations should happen the moment an issue arises. But research from Dr. John Gottman shows that how a conversation begins predicts how it will end 96 percent of the time. In other words, timing and tone matter as much as the topic itself.

A harsh startup, filled with blame, criticism, or launched when a partner is distracted or emotionally flooded, almost always leads to escalation. Even reasonable concerns can turn into fights when the nervous system is already on high alert.

A soft startup works differently. It includes getting consent, choosing the right moment, and setting the stage before diving in. This approach lowers defensiveness and makes collaboration possible.

This chapter is a guide to the soft startup. The goal is to create the conditions where you can actually be heard.

Step 1: Get Consent for the Conversation

Consent applies to more than physical intimacy; it's essential for emotional intimacy. Asking, "Is this a good time to talk?" shows respect for your partner's availability and sets the stage for a productive exchange.

If your partner says no, resist the urge to push. Instead, ask, "When would be a good time to talk about this?"

Here's the key: the partner who says, "Not now," takes on two responsibilities:

▶ They must offer an alternate time within twenty-four hours.

▶ They must be the one to bring the conversation back up at that time.

This follow-through is essential for building trust.

A Note for Turtles: This step can be difficult if you are inclined to avoid conflict. You may feel reluctant to reopen a topic once things feel calm. But honoring the agreement to revisit the conversation is essential. Avoiding it may feel easier in the moment, but it erodes trust and safety over time.

Step 2: Clarify the Topic

Effective conversations don't happen in a fog of confusion. Before starting, identify the specific topic you want to address and frame it around your feelings and needs; not a generalized complaint.

▶ **Ineffective:** "We need to talk about everything that's wrong."

▶ **Effective:** "I want to talk about how I've been feeling disconnected lately and what we might do to feel closer."

This clarity helps the conversation stay focused and prevents it from spiraling into unrelated issues.

Step 3: Run the Pre-Conversation Checklist

Once you have a time and a topic, you must ensure the conditions are right. Before you begin, check these three things:

▶ **Are Both Partners Sober and Drug-Free?**
Substances can cloud judgment, amplify emotions, and make meaningful dialogue impossible. Save heart-to-heart conversations for times when you are both clear-headed.

▶ **Do We Have 45-60 Minutes of Uninterrupted Time?**
Meaningful conversations take time. Attempting to rush or multitask sends the message that the conversation isn't a priority. Clear your schedules and turn off distractions.

▶ **Are Both Partners Emotionally Regulated?**
This is the most important check. Emotional regulation means being in a state where you can listen without defensiveness and speak without attacking. If emotions are already running high (a 7-10 on the Scale of Distress), you are in "Wildfire" mode and cannot have a productive talk.

If you are dysregulated, take at least twenty minutes to calm your nervous system (take a walk, breathe, listen to music) before you try to engage.

Step 4: The Readiness Test (The Final Gateway)

You've set a time, you have a topic, and you're both regulated. This is the final check-in. The Readiness Test confirms that you are both emotionally prepared and willing to do the work.

State these three affirmations out loud to each other:

▶ **"I agree to stay on script."** (This means I will follow the steps, like reflecting, and not bring up unrelated topics.)

▶ **"I want to understand you."** (This shows my genuine desire to hear your perspective, not just "win.")

▶ **"I am emotionally regulated."** (I am calm and in control, ready to engage without reacting defensively.)

Briefly Hold Hands

Once you have both said these statements, reach for each other's hand. This physical touchpoint sends a powerful cue of safety to each other's nervous system. It reassures you both that you are safe and it is okay to be vulnerable.

If holding hands feels tense, or one of you can't do it, that's a sign. It indicates one or both of you is still not truly regulated or ready. You must pause and take more time.

What Is the "Right Mindset?"

Think of the Readiness Test as what gets you into the conversation. The Right Mindset is the spirit you bring once you're there.

It is not complicated. It is just you saying, in your own quiet way, "I am here to understand you, not to win."

It sounds like this:

- ▶ I will listen without jumping in.
- ▶ I will put my assumptions on the shelf for a minute.
- ▶ I will repeat back what I hear to be sure I have it right.
- ▶ I will keep an eye on my own reactions.
- ▶ I will take responsibility for what I feel and what I need.

That is really it.

Starting well is less about choosing the perfect words and more about choosing the posture you want to bring. When you begin a conversation with this mindset, you create the kind of space where real connection has a chance to show up.

"Raise your words,
not your voice. It is rain
that grows flowers,
not thunder."

- RUMI

CHAPTER 13

Sticking to the Script

When a conversation gets difficult, it's easy to fall into destructive patterns of miscommunication: blaming, defending, shutting down, or bringing up old wounds. When this happens, you move from understanding each other to simply trying to win the argument or end the discomfort.

This chapter is about shifting that pattern. When emotions run high, the instinct is to react automatically. But reaction rarely leads to resolution. The key to *all* effective Wholehearted Communication (whether Level 1, 2, or 3) is learning to slow down, regulate, and stay engaged without falling into old habits.

This chapter outlines specific strategies that will help you:

▶ Recognize when you're emotionally overwhelmed and regulate.

▶ Stay present instead of shutting down.

▶ Use structured language to prevent misunderstandings.

▶ Shift from proving a point to creating mutual understanding.

▶ Break out of repetitive cycles of conflict.

These techniques are your toolkit for turning even the most difficult conversations into opportunities for deeper connection.

Rules for the Road

We all know the feeling. You're in a discussion, and within minutes you're back in a familiar pattern. One person starts talking faster. The other pulls away. The conversation shifts from understanding to self-protection.

For some couples, that looks like chilly silence and avoiding "going there." These are two turtles.

For others, it looks like chaos and volatility. Two bees. Either way, nothing gets resolved. The pattern takes over.

These breakdowns don't happen because you don't love each other. They happen because when emotions rise, old patterns take over. Sometimes that looks like escalation. Sometimes it looks like shutdown.

But what if, instead of getting stuck, you had a way to slow things down, stay connected, and actually hear each other?

If you're already feeling a little overwhelmed, that makes sense. This is a lot of information, and it may be very different from how you're used to having conversations. You are not expected to do all of this at once, or to do it perfectly.

Think of what follows as a menu, not a checklist. Some of these ideas will land right away. Others will make more sense later. Simply becoming aware of one or two of them is more than enough to start changing how conversations unfold.

Take a breath. You're not behind. You're exactly where you need to be.

Slowing Down Changes Everything

A deep breath. A pause before jumping in. These small choices change the entire direction of a conversation. Everything in you will want to speed up or shut down when you feel misunderstood. Speeding up and shutting down look different, but they come from the same place. Both are nervous system responses to feeling overwhelmed. Slowing down is what interrupts them.

The Power of Eye Contact

In tense moments, it's easy to look away. And sometimes you need to, especially if you're trying not to get overwhelmed. But when you can stay visually connected, even briefly, it helps your partner feel you're still in the room with them. Eye contact says, "I'm here. I'm listening." If eye contact is too much, aim for their face, their forehead, or even just turning your body toward them. The goal is presence, not intensity.

Why There Are No Questions

This part often surprises people.

If you are used to clarifying, checking understanding, or asking questions to stay connected, Wholehearted Communication can feel strange at first. A common response is, *"But how do I understand what my partner means if I can't ask questions?"*

There are no questions by design.

In the middle of a charged conversation, questions usually come from discomfort. Fear. Worry. Hurt. They are often an attempt to settle your nervous system, correct a story forming in your mind, or move the conversation forward before there is enough shared understanding.

That impulse is human.

But it shifts the focus away from connection and toward control.

Wholehearted Communication is not about pulling information out of your partner. It is about letting them actually see you. It is the mutual revealing of feelings and needs, not an exchange of explanations or defenses.

So when you notice the urge to ask a question, pause to progress.

That urge is information.

Instead of asking, turn inward and notice:

- ▶ What am I afraid is true right now?
- ▶ What story am I telling myself?
- ▶ What am I feeling in my body?
- ▶ What am I needing underneath this reaction?

Then share that.

Not as an accusation.
Not as a rebuttal.
Not as a solution.

Just as a revealing.

For example, instead of asking:

"Why didn't you just remind me?"
"Are you saying I never follow through?"
"What exactly do you want me to do differently?"

You might say:

"What I make up is that you see me as unreliable or not pulling my weight.

When I tell myself that story, I feel defensive and ashamed at the same time. My chest tightens, and I notice an urge to explain myself or shut down.

Underneath that, I'm needing understanding and some grace, because I already feel like I'm failing in a lot of areas right now."

No questions.
No rebuttal.
No explanation yet.

Just revealing.

This is what keeps a conversation grounded in connection instead of strategy. When we ask questions, we're often trying to calm our own anxiety or get our partner to fix the story we're telling ourselves. When we reveal what's happening inside us, we give our partner something real to understand.

Over time, something important happens.

When both partners consistently share what they are making up, how they feel, and what they need, the questions that once felt necessary often answer themselves. Understanding emerges not because it was demanded, but because it was made safe.

This can feel awkward at first. That's expected. Staying with your own experience long enough to share it clearly builds skill. With practice, you'll notice less escalation and more understanding.

Follow the Script

We've all been there. A conversation about the trash turns into a conversation about everything. Once past issues start coming up, the original topic is usually gone. That's when things start to spiral.

Sticking to the script means staying focused on this conversation and this topic. If something from the past still needs to be addressed, it deserves its own conversation at another time.

Keep It Short (The 2-Minute Rule)

Some people process by talking. Others shut down when there's too much information at once. The goal is to keep each "send" brief and focused on one point. That gives your partner a better chance to actually hear you, not just plan a response.

If this is hard, a two-minute timer can help. Think of it as training wheels, not a punishment.

For bees, the work is saying less. Two minutes is usually plenty.

For turtles, the work is saying more. Use the full two minutes. Put words to what's happening inside you, even if it feels awkward or unfinished.

Different nervous systems need different guardrails. The timer helps both partners stay in the conversation.

Conversations Should Have a Time Limit

A two-hour conversation rarely leads to clarity. More often, it leads to exhaustion.

When you're first learning Wholehearted Communication, set a 90-minute limit. If you're not finished, take a 24-hour break and come back to it later. Pushing past the point of fatigue increases tension and makes it harder to stay grounded.

Stopping is not quitting. It's protecting the conversation.

As mentioned earlier, by your tenth conversation, many couples notice they no longer need the full 90 minutes. For couples with higher nervous system reactivity, it may take 20 or 30 conversations. The number itself isn't what matters.

What matters is that you're building skills that reduce negativity, shorten conflict, increase understanding, and help you find your way back to each other more quickly. Expect a greater investment of time at the beginning, and trust that the time required will decrease as these skills become more familiar.

Some Conversations Need More Than One Round

"I think we've made progress, and I'd like to check in again tomorrow after dinner."

Or after the kids go to bed. Or over coffee in the morning. The exact timing matters less than the clarity. What matters is knowing when the conversation will return.

Leaving a conversation with a plan gives both of you something to lean on. It adds predictability at a time when things can otherwise feel unsettled. The issue is tabled, not ignored. You're not pretending it doesn't exist. You're agreeing not to work on it right now.

An unresolved issue does not require constant tension. You don't have to keep the conflict alive by acting irritated, withdrawn, or distant so no one forgets there's still something to talk about. You can set the issue aside and still enjoy each other and your life together.

Learning how to move in and out of conflict is a powerful relational skill. It develops when couples create protected space to talk about hard things, feel what they feel, say what needs to be said, and then close the conversation intentionally. Not with a solution, but with a plan.

Until then, you get to go back to being a couple. The issue will still be there when you return to it.

Owning Your Story Instead of Assigning Theirs

Blame is the quickest way to shut down a conversation.

- **Ineffective (Blame):** "You always make me feel invisible."
- **Effective (Own Your Story):** "I feel invisible when decisions are made without my opinion, and the story I make up is that my opinion doesn't matter."

Owning your story keeps the conversation grounded in your experience. Your feelings are where connection begins.

The Role of Gratitude in Tough Conversations

It might feel unnatural, but starting with appreciation is a great way to start a conversation. "I really appreciate how much you care about this, and I want to understand your perspective." This sets a tone that you are on the same team.

What to Do When Your Protector is Running the Show

You might shift into self-protection. The signs are easy to recognize:

▶ You're narrating your partner's experience ("You're upset because you think I don't care.")

▶ You're defending yourself instead of listening ("I only said that because you started it.")

▶ You're justifying your actions ("I didn't mean to hurt you; I was just tired.")

▶ You're dysregulated, reactive, and just thinking about your comeback.

When you notice these things, pause to progress. Take a breath. Ask yourself, "What do I need to understand here?"

If you're feeling flooded just reading this, that's a sign this tool is relevant for you. It's here to slow things down and help you come back online, not to give you another thing to do perfectly.

TOOL: The BEST Test (When You Get Activated)

This is the tool to use when you feel yourself getting activated *in the middle* of a conversation. You can pause the conversation and say, "I need to do the BEST Test before we go any further."

This is a self-regulating exercise to bring awareness to what's happening inside you.

▶ **B – Body:** Describe the sensations. "I'm noticing that my heart is racing and my chest feels tight."

▶ **E – Emotions:** Name your feelings. "I feel anxious and frustrated, like I'm on the verge of snapping."

▶ **S – Stories:** Describe the story you're telling yourself. "The story I'm telling myself is that you don't trust me and think I'm irresponsible."

▶ **T – Truth:** Challenge your story with facts. "The truth is, you haven't said that. You just said you want to stay on track. I am projecting my own fears onto you."

This pause helps you come back with more clarity, so you can stay in the conversation without turning it into a fight or a shutdown.

Transforming Conversations, Strengthening Relationships

Wholehearted Communication is a practice. Keep the scripts accessible. Save it to your phone. It's necessary to rely on the script while you're learning. With time, it becomes less about following prompts and more about embodying the principles of connection, empathy, and vulnerability.

But the script is only half the battle. Our bodies are communicating long before we ever open our mouths. In the next chapter, we'll explore the world of non-verbal communication. These are the cues you're sending, whether you mean to or not.

"What you do speaks so loudly that I cannot hear what you say."

— RALPH WALDO EMERSON

CHAPTER 14

Non-Verbal

The Cues You're Sending

"If looks could kill…"

Yep, that's nonverbal communication in action. You don't need words to feel someone's energy shift. That glare? That sigh? That eye roll? We pick up on so much without anyone saying a thing.

Sometimes a sigh means, *I'm tired.* Sometimes it means, *I'm irritated.* Sometimes it means, *I've heard this before and I'm waiting for my turn.*

The problem isn't what the sigh means. The problem is that nothing gets said out loud.

The partner who's talking often fills in the blanks quickly. *I'm boring you. You don't care. I should stop.* They trail off or shut down. Meanwhile, the partner who sighed may be thinking, *I just want a turn,* or *We're going in circles,* without realizing how loudly their body spoke.

This is how people miss each other without meaning to. One person reacts to what they felt. The other reacts to what they meant. And neither names it.

Cues of Safety and the Feedback Loop

Happy couples are good at positive nonverbal cues. They send more positive signals: warm smiles, affectionate touches, and nods of understanding. Just as importantly, they *notice* and *receive* those signals. As we defined in Chapter

7, these are cues of safety. When partners receive cues of safety regularly, it creates a positive emotional feedback loop.

But when a couple is struggling, those cues start to change. Eye contact becomes less frequent. Voices can flatten or turn sharp. Body language closes off in small but noticeable ways, like crossed arms, turned backs, or heavier sighs. At that point, both nervous systems are already on edge, watching for the next sign that something might go wrong.

Just as negative body language can quietly derail a conversation, cues of safety can steady it. Often, they're more effective than words.

A kind glance. A softer tone. A hand reached out instead of pulled away. These signals tell your partner, *I'm here. I'm not going anywhere.* They help the nervous system settle before anything logical has a chance to register.

When couples learn to use these cues intentionally, conversations feel less brittle. There's more room to speak, more willingness to listen, and less urgency to defend or withdraw. The words matter, but the body often sets the tone first.

Small changes in how you show up physically can create meaningful shifts in connection, sometimes faster than anything you could say.

The Power of What's Unspoken

Eye contact, facial expressions, and body language are all part of how we connect. But it's crucial to remember that there is no one-size-fits-all approach.

▶ **Eye Contact:** For many, a few extra seconds of eye contact signals emotional presence. For others, or in some cultures, it can feel uncomfortable or disrespectful. The goal is not to stare, but to let your partner feel seen in a way that feels respectful to *both* of you.

▶ **Style:** Some people are physically expressive, leaning in or using touch to show they're listening. Others are more subtle, showing they're engaged through a softening of their tone.

▶ **Sensation:** One partner may feel comforted by touch during a difficult conversation (a hand on the knee), while the other may find it distracting and prefer to connect through words first.

When partners have different nonverbal styles, it's easy to misread each other. One of you might be more expressive, the other more reserved. That doesn't mean one of you cares more. It just means you're communicating in different ways.

A Dictionary of Cues

We are all constantly sending silent messages. Paying attention to them is the first step in communicating more consciously.

Nonverbal Cues that Bring You Together

These cues build bridges and create safety.

Cues That Bring You Together (Bridges)

▶ **Facial expressions**: A real smile or a soft gaze that says, "I see you."
▶ **Body posture:** An open, relaxed posture that invites connection.
▶ **Gestures:** A nod or a hand on a knee that says, "You are not alone."
▶ **Tone of voice:** A calm, steady tone that invites safety.

Cues That Pull You Apart (Walls)

▶ **Eye rolling:** This sends a clear message of contempt.
▶ **Turning away:** This can feel like turning away from the relationship itself.
▶ **Tense posture:** Crossed arms or clenched fists show you are "armored up."
▶ **Heavy sighing:** This often communicates, "I give up" or "You are exhausting."

The Real Task: From "Acting Out" to "Speaking Out"

Nonverbal cues are easy to miss when we are stressed. They are often the first place disconnection shows up.

All emotions are felt privately, and you either decide what to do with them, or your nervous system decides for you. Many people learn early on that their feelings are too much, don't matter, or won't be considered. Over time, you may form silent agreements with yourself to keep emotions tucked away.

You might withdraw, shut down, lash out, or become overly accommodating. These are all ways of *acting out* emotions instead of *speaking* them.

The problem is, when you act out feelings, your partner is left to guess what is going on. This creates confusion and distance. The goal is to stop performing emotions and start sharing them.

Being able to feel, stay with, and express your experience in words that support connection is a skill. It takes courage to share what's real, especially if life has taught you that it's safer not to. But your emotions are the key to being understood.

And the thing about feelings is, you will have them, whether you name them or not. They exist. They are real. The most important thing you can do is treat them like they matter.

"When a couple argues,
they're usually not even in
the same fight."

- ERMA BOMBECK

CHAPTER 15

LEVEL 1

No-Fault Formula

Level 1: Clearing the "Smoke"

Before we dive in, it's essential to understand that Wholehearted Communication is a structured, level-based system. It's not meant for casual daily chatter or open-ended personal sharing. Instead, it offers a framework for open-hearted conversations designed to help you and your partner manage moments of disconnection as they arise.

Level 1 is the most common and accessible level of conversation in Wholehearted Communication.

Think of Level 1 as a tool for clearing the "smoke" of miscommunication before it turns into fire. It isn't meant for digging into deep-seated problems; that's when you need Level 2 or Level 3. A Level 1 conversation is a simple and proactive check-in that helps prevent small misunderstandings. It is used to bring something up that matters to you before it becomes a conflict.

Recognizing When a Level 1 Conversation is Needed

A Level 1 conversation is needed when your goal is to clarify or express a thought, feeling, or need before it turns into a conflict or hurt.

Signs it's time for a Level 1 conversation:

▶ You're feeling something and want to share it without blame or urgency.

▶ You notice you're starting to make up a story about your partner's behavior.

▶ There's a small misunderstanding or tension that could grow if left unspoken.

▶ You want to bring something up that matters to you, but it's not a conflict ...yet.

▶ You're unsure if your partner knows what you're feeling, needing, or intending.

▶ You've noticed a pattern you'd like to draw attention to in a responsible and intentional way.

The Goal: Connection, Not Correction

The goal of Level 1 is to be proactive, not reactive. It's an attempt to stay ahead of misunderstandings and keep the relationship "emotionally clean."

You're aiming for connection, not correction. Course-correcting in real-time to clear up assumptions stops tiny sparks from becoming big fires and keeps your relationship in sync.

How to Initiate a Level 1 Conversation

Once you notice a disconnect or sign of "smoke," a Level 1 response starts with the No-Fault Formula (NFF).

This is a scripted statement that provides guardrails to keep your conversation safe, clear, and productive, creating a balanced rhythm where both of you can be heard without defensiveness or misinterpretation.

When couples first try these scripts, reactions vary widely. Some feel immediate relief. Others feel awkward, mechanical, or resistant. All of these responses are normal.

The more you practice, the more natural it feels. Over time, it doesn't just help you avoid conflict; it builds a foundation where trust and connection grow.

Let's look at the specific steps involved in a Level 1 Conversation using the No-Fault Formula.

Some people make sense of things by reading and reflecting. Others need to *see it laid out visually. If you're a visual learner, you'll find diagrams at the end of the chapter that map out the concepts introduced here.*

Identify Your Roles

Whether you are experiencing frustration or hurt or noticing your partner's negative emotions, either of you can initiate step 1. The person who initiates the conversation is the Sender and the other is the Receiver.

Step 1: The Sender Shares (The Invitation)

This is the No-Fault Formula that is used to effectively introduce a topic or concern.

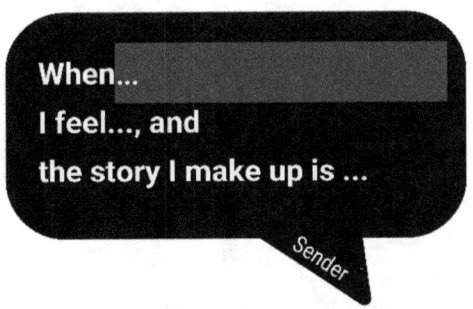

Wholehearted Communication is rooted in the belief that what we most want in relationships is to invite our partner to care. That invitation begins with how you open the conversation.

If you leave this first step up to your nervous system, it will often come out sounding like a sneak attack: sharp, defensive, or critical. But when you pause to use the No-Fault Formula, you create a safe and sincere opening. You're saying to your partner, "Here's what I experienced, here's how it felt, and here's the story I told myself about it."

This gives your partner a clear window into your inner world without putting them on the defensive.

Without the No-Fault Formula

▶ **Ineffective Defensive Start:** "You're always on your phone at dinner. You don't even care about me anymore." (This start sparks an argument.)

With the No-Fault Formula

▶ **Effective (Inviting them to Care):** "When you check your phone during dinner, I feel unimportant, and the story I make up is that I'm not a priority." (This invites the Receiver to understand their experience.)

Step 2: The Receiver Reflects (The Fact-Check)

The Receiver's only job is to reflect what they heard without debating, defending, or correcting. This step, which we call Fact-Checking, confirms whether the message sent was the message received, not whether it was accurate or justified.

What I hear you saying is...

Did I get it?

Receiver

Continuing the Example:

- ▶ **Receiver:** "What I hear you saying is that when I'm on my phone during dinner, it leaves you feeling unimportant and like you're not a priority. Did I get it?"

Step 3: The Sender Confirms, Clarifies, or Corrects

After the Receiver reflects back what they heard, the Sender checks to see if the message was received as intended.

- ▶ If **yes**, a simple "Yes, you got it" lets both people know the message landed.
- ▶ If **no**, the Sender gently clarifies or corrects it.

This "process-not-performance" approach gives space to say, "That's what I said, but not quite what I meant," and try again with more accuracy.

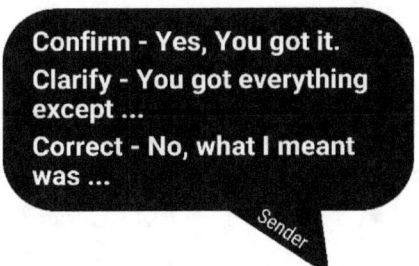

Confirm - Yes, You got it.
Clarify - You got everything except ...
Correct - No, what I meant was ...

Sender

Example of Clarifying

- ▶ **Sender:** "I'm frustrated that you're on your phone so much."
  Receiver: "You're upset that I'm always on my phone. Did I get it?"

- ▶ **Sender:** "Sort of. It's not *always*. It's mostly at dinner, when I want us to connect. That's what I meant."
  Receiver: "Okay, so it's not that I am always on my phone, just at dinner, and that's when you want more connection with me. Did I get it?"

- ▶ **Sender:** "Yes, you got it."

Step 4: The Receiver Reflects Until Confirmed

This is the "lather, rinse, repeat" step. The Receiver continues to reflect the Sender's clarifications until the Sender finally confirms, "Yes, you got it." This back-and-forth is not a sign of failure; it's the definition of success.

Example of Repeating Until Confirmed

- **Sender:** "I felt embarrassed at the party when you teased me in front of our friends."
  Receiver: "What I hear you saying is that you were mad at me for making a joke at the party. Did I get it?"

- **Sender:** "No, not mad, more embarrassed. It felt like I was the punchline."
  Receiver: "Okay, you weren't angry, you were embarrassed because the joke made you feel like the punchline. Did I get it?"

- **Sender:** "Yes, you got it."

Step 5: The Receiver Asks, "Is There More on This Point?"

Once the message has been confirmed, the Receiver asks this simple question. It signals curiosity and a commitment to fully understanding their partner's experience. It also keeps the conversation on track.

Is there more on that point?

Receiver

Example of "Is There More?"

▶ **Sender:** "When you left without saying goodbye this morning, I felt invisible, and the story I made up is that I don't matter to you."
Receiver: "What I hear you saying is that you felt invisible, like you didn't matter, when I left without saying goodbye. Did I get it?"

▶ **Sender:** "Yes. You got it."
Receiver: "Is there more on that point?"

▶ **Sender:** "Yes, really, what I am trying to say is that lately I have been feeling this way more and more, and each time I get that feeling it's worse and worse."
Receiver: "So, what I hear you saying is that you also want me to know that this has happened more and more recently, and that adds to the hurt. Did I get it?"

▶ **Sender:** "Yes, you got it."
Receiver: "Is there more on that point?"

▶ **Sender:** "No, that's it for this point."

Step 6: Switch Roles (Validate, Then Share)

When the Sender has nothing more to add to their point, the roles switch. The New Sender (the original Receiver) now has two jobs. This is the most important "turn" in the entire conversation.

Part 1: Validate

First, the New Sender validates what they just heard. This step matters more than most people realize, and it's also where many conversations break down. Not because people don't care, but because validation often feels counterintuitive. When emotions are activated, the instinct is to explain, defend, fix, or reassure. Validation asks you to pause all of that.

Validation is the bridge that makes it possible for the original Sender to truly listen. This means putting yourself in your partner's shoes and letting their experience register, even if you see the situation differently. You are essentially saying, "It makes sense to me that you feel the way you do."

Validation does not require agreement. It does not mean you think your partner is right. It simply means you are willing to pause your own perspective long enough to fully consider theirs. You cannot overdo this. Validate. Validate. Validate.

> **It makes sense that you feel/see it that way because...**
>
> *New Sender*

▸ **New Sender (Part 1: Validating):** "It makes total sense that you'd feel dismissed. I did pick up my phone while you were talking, and I can see how that would send a message of disinterest. You wanted my full attention, and my action made it seem like you didn't matter. I can see how that would hurt."
New Receiver (Original Sender): "Yes, thank you for getting that."

Notice what's missing here. There's no defending. No explaining. No justification. Just an acknowledgment of how the experience felt.

Common Validation Mistakes

Before moving on, it's important to name a few ways validation often goes off track:

▸ **Validating and then immediately defending:**
"I get why you were upset, but..."

- ▸ **Reassurance disguised as validation:**
  "You don't need to feel that way."
- ▸ **Explaining instead of acknowledging:**
  "I only picked up my phone for a second."
- ▸ **Rushing through validation to get to your turn:**
  Treating validation like a formality instead of understanding.

If your partner doesn't feel understood yet, you're not done validating.

Part 2: Share.

Only after validation is complete does the New Sender share their own key point about the same situation. Using the prompt "How I see it is..." the New Sender reveals their perspective and feelings about the topic. Then they pause, allowing their partner (the New Receiver) to reflect.

- ▸ **New Sender (Part 2: Sharing their perspective):** "How I see it is ..., I had no idea I was doing it, and that worries me. I don't want to be the partner who is checked out at dinner with you."

Step 7: Repeat the Cycle

Now the roles reverse. The New Receiver reflects, confirms, and asks "Is there more?" When the Sender has nothing more to add, roles switch. Each time roles switch, the New Sender validates first: "It makes sense that you feel..." and only then shares their own perspective: "How I see it is..." This cycle continues, one point at a time, until both partners feel fully heard.

See the Level 1 diagram on the following page for a visual of this cycle.

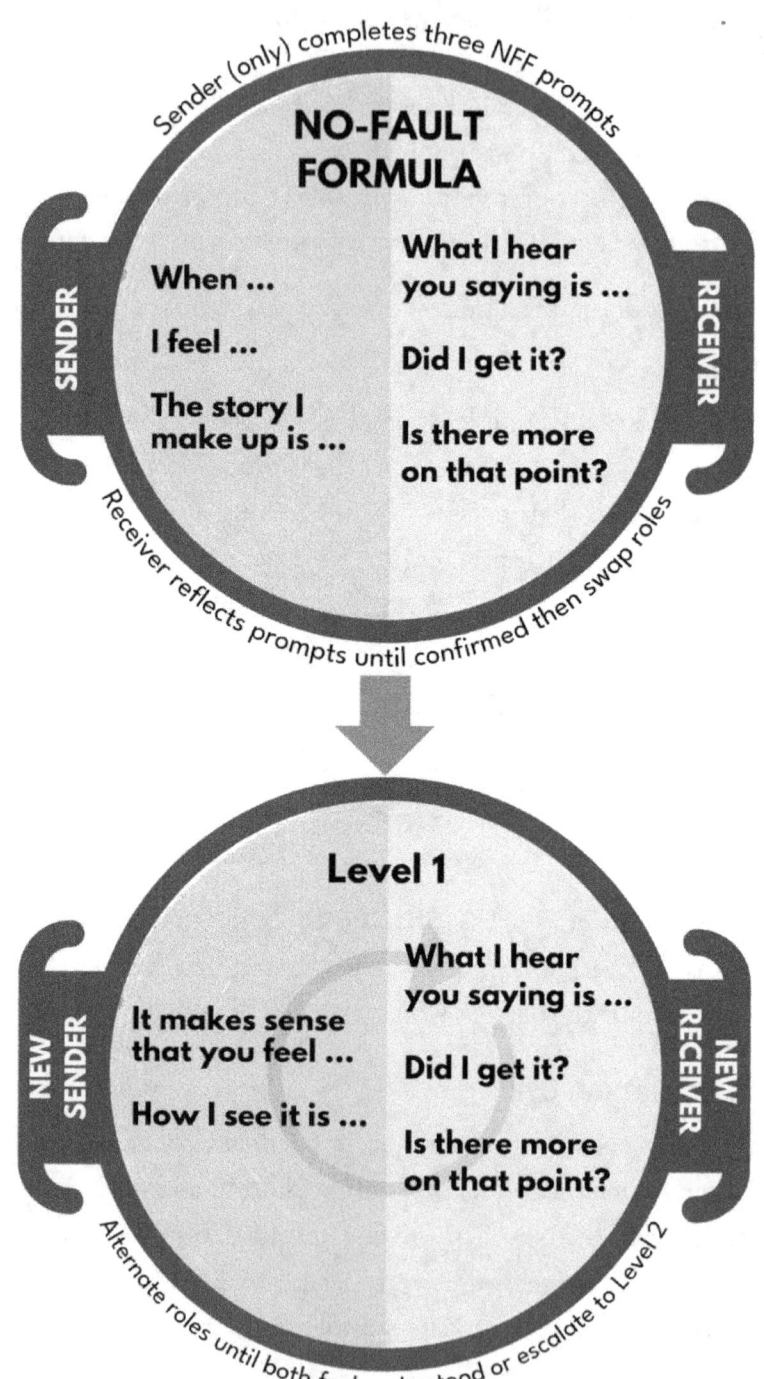

Level 1: Rules for the Road

This scripted process can be hard. Your nervous system will want to interrupt, defend, or shut down. Here is how to handle the most common challenges.

1. **For the Sender: Stick to "Manageable Pieces"**

   As the Sender, you may feel the urge to explain everything at once. But your partner can only take in so much. To stay connected, you must share in manageable pieces (about 1-2 minutes at most). Trust that you will have a voice.

2. **For the Receiver: Give "Wiggle Room"**

   Your partner may sound robotic or distant as they reflect. It's possible they are activated and are using all their energy just to stay present and follow the script. Instead of criticizing their delivery, give them "wiggle room" for trying. Effort matters.

3. **For Everyone: Don't "Tone Police"**

   It's tempting to correct *how* your partner is speaking. But as soon as you shift from *what* is being said to *how* it's being said, the conversation turns from connection to criticism. Instead of correcting their tone, steer the conversation back to the core message.

4. **For the Receiver: "Empty" When You're Full**

   As the Receiver, your mind might start looping, or your emotions may feel too big to hold. You can't listen if you're "full." This is when you need "to empty." Kindly raise your hand and say, "I need to pause you here so I can empty." This alerts your partner that you need a moment to breathe and self-regulate before you can truly listen again. This is not avoidance; it's effective listening.

5. **For Everyone: Take a Break When You're Flooded**

   If "emptying" isn't enough, you may be approaching your "Wildfire" zone. If your heart starts to race, anyone can call for a break. Try saying: "I'm noticing my chest tightening right now. I think I need a quick break to reset. Can we pick this back up in ten minutes?"

Asking for a break is not giving up. It's essential self-care that prevents you from causing more harm. It's counterintuitive, but the slower you go, the faster you understand each other.

No-Fault Communication Cycle

When combined, these steps create the No-Fault Communication Cycle, which is synonymous with a Level 1 Wholehearted Communication.

But knowing *how* to use this tool is only half the battle; we also need to know *when* and *why*.

Finding the Balance: Turtles and Bumblebees

A well-timed check-in stops tiny sparks from turning into a full-blown fire. But checking in too often can backfire, turning connection into an emotional treadmill, where one partner feels drained and the other feels pressured. I've watched couples who initially resisted the structure begin to rely on it during harder conversations, not because it feels natural at first, but because it helps them stay connected when emotions spike.

The key is balance, and this is where partners often struggle.

> ▶ **Turtles tell themselves**: *I'll wait until I have something important to say.* They hesitate too much. But little misunderstandings don't just disappear. By the time the Turtle is ready to talk, the moment may have passed, and their partner might have already felt the distance. Over time, this erodes trust as their partner thinks, *They don't care, and I always have to reach out.*
> ▶ **Bumblebees tell themselves**: *I need to talk about this right now.* They check in too much. But these rapid-fire check-ins can leave their partner feeling overwhelmed, defensive, or exhausted rather than connected.

Take Casey and Quinn. Casey (a Bumblebee) used to check in constantly, wanting reassurance at every little shift. At first, it felt helpful, but it became exhausting for both of them.

Eventually, Casey learned to pause and ask the most important question of Level 1:

> "Am I seeking connection, or am I seeking reassurance to manage my own anxiety?"

If the urge feels more about your internal state of fear or insecurity, try self-soothing first. But if it still feels relational, that is your cue to initiate a Level 1 conversation. When you check in with intention instead of impulse, you strengthen the connection instead of draining it.

Connection vs. Reassurance

Here are examples to help you recognize the difference.

Check-ins Driven by Anxiety (Reassurance-Seeking)

These are often about calming your own inner anxiety. The goal is to reduce your *own* distress, not to create connection. Reassurance-seeking might sound like:

> "Are you mad at me?" "Are we okay?" "Why didn't you respond to my text?" "I feel like you've been distant. Is something wrong with us?" "You're not leaving me, are you?"

Check-ins Driven by Connection (The No-Fault Formula)

These stem from a desire to understand, share, and care for the relationship. You are not asking your partner to manage your feelings; you are sharing your feelings so they can understand you.

Reassurance-seeking is not the only way anxiety shows up. Sometimes it comes out soft and pleading, and other times it comes out sharp and blaming.

Both responses are driven by the same thing: a nervous system looking for relief.

The examples below illustrate how to turn any anxiety-driven start, whether it sounds soft like "Are you mad at me?" or sharp like "What's your problem?", into a connection-driven check-in by using the No-Fault Formula.

The point is not that every example here is reassurance-seeking. The point is that both reassurance and criticism are attempts to manage discomfort rather than create connection. Using the No-Fault Formula (NFF) shifts the conversation from getting relief to creating understanding.

- ▶ **Ineffective:** "What's your problem, why were you so snappy earlier?"
  NFF: "When your tone feels tense, I feel anxious, and the story I make up is that I did something to upset you."
- ▶ **Ineffective:** "We never spend time together anymore."
  NFF: "When we go a while without slowing down together, I feel lonely, and the story I make up is that maybe you do not miss me the same way I miss you."
- ▶ **Ineffective:** "You are always too busy to listen to me."
  NFF: "When you seem busy or distracted, I feel hesitant, and the story I make up is that what I have to say will not matter to you."
- ▶ **Ineffective:** "You never make time for me unless I force it."
  NFF: "When we carve out time together, I feel close and secure, and the story I make up is that we could keep growing stronger if we made this a habit."

An Invitation, Not a Demand

The No-Fault Formula is about opening a window and letting your partner see what's going on inside of you. It's a way of sharing, not prying.

Instead of asking questions or fishing for answers, you're offering your own feelings. It's about saying, "Here's what's happening for me," rather than, "What's going on with you?"

That simple shift makes all the difference. Sharing this way creates closeness instead of distance, understanding instead of defensiveness, and connection instead of criticism. When you lead with connection, your check-in becomes an invitation instead of a demand.

A Note for the Partner (When You're Sought for Reassurance)

If your partner frequently seeks reassurance, it's natural to want to comfort them. But always being the one to soothe can unintentionally create a cycle of dependency.

Instead of jumping in with, "We're fine, don't worry," try gently redirecting the conversation toward connection. You might ask:

> "Can you help me understand what you are experiencing that causes you to question if we are okay?"

This kind of response invites your partner to slow down and reflect, rather than slipping into an automatic reassurance loop. It shifts the focus from a quick fix for anxiety to exploring what's really going on, together.

When Level 1 Isn't Enough

A No-Fault Formula conversation sometimes reveals that the issue runs deeper. The "smoke" is coming from a "fire." When this happens, either the Sender or the Receiver can transition to Level 2 when it is their turn to speak.

This shift is as simple as using the phrases:

> "How we see this the same..."
> and,
> "How we see this differently..."

These prompts naturally guide the conversation into the deeper exploration required for a Level 2 conversation. Next, we'll dive into how to transition from a Level 1 to a Level 2 conversation.

WHOLEHEARTED COMMUNICATION

LEVEL 1 **LEVEL 1**

Miscommunication & Minor Disagreements

Level 1 conversations are meant to resolve misunderstandings as they occur, with either person able to initiate.

S SENDER　　　　**R RECEIVER**

No-Fault Formula

When [facts/not stories],
I feel [feeling word], and
The story I make up is...
Correct/Clarify/Confirm
Yes, you got it.
No, you forgot...
What I meant was...

If clarification or
correction is needed,
continue as the sender.
If confirmed, swap roles;
the receiver now validates
and shares.

Fact Check
What I hear you saying ...
Did I get it?
Is there more on that point?

**Continue Reflecting
Until Confirmed**

Swap Roles ☝

Validate
It makes sense you feel/
see it that way because...

Share
How I feel/see it is...

Fact Check
What I hear you saying ...
Did I get it?
Is there more on that point?

Correct/Clarify/Confirm
Yes, you got it.
No, you forgot...
What I meant was...

Keep Swapping Roles Until You Both Feel Understood
If unable to reach an understanding, proceed to Level 2.

Slow down, maintain eye contact, and take turns to prevent escalation. Limit each turn to one minute, focus on facts, and own your stories. Use phrases like "On the one hand..." and "On the other hand..." for opposing truths. Focus on your internal experience and avoid asking questions.

lesbianloveadv.com

183

"*Clear is kind.*
Unclear is unkind."

- BRENÉ BROWN

CHAPTER 16

When a Level 1 Conversation Becomes a Level 2 Conversation

Level 1 is about catching tension early, using reflection and validation to prevent escalation, and keeping communication on track. It's a process of back-and-forth structured sharing that allows both partners to feel heard and understood.

Level 2 is an entirely different kind of conversation. Rather than focusing on sharing and clarifying, Level 2 is about sorting facts and feelings while narrowing the focus to the heart of the matter.

The Table

Instead of continuing the open-ended exchange used in Level 1, you'll shift to placing *one point at a time* on the Table.

This is where things become more structured and intentional. The Table is symbolic. It represents two people coming together, face-to-face as if seated at a table with a shared purpose: to sort through misunderstandings, align with each other around shared truths, and address emotional disconnection with clarity and care. This isn't about debating who's right. It's about working together, one step at a time, to restore connection.

The goal is to untangle the parts where you already agree from the issues you see differently. Rather than circling around the same frustrations, this stage brings order to the conversation, helping both partners see what still feels unclear or unresolved in the same way. It's about making sense of the emotions and perspectives at play.

The Heart of the Matter

Level 2 serves an even deeper purpose: identifying the heart of the matter. What is causing the pain that keeps us in this dance? What is beneath the surface of this disagreement that makes it feel so charged? Often, it's not just about the topic itself but about what it represents, the deeper fears, unmet needs, or past experiences.

It is also about finding our way back to each other, even when we don't see things the same way. Instead of needing agreement to feel safe, we shift toward the security that comes from knowing we can hold space for each other's differences without shaking the foundation of our relationship.

This process moves us from reactivity to understanding, from feeling at odds to recognizing that we are on the same team. And just to be clear, moving to Level 2 doesn't mean Level 1 failed. It's an intentional step toward a deeper understanding when things need more structure.

When Level 1 Becomes Level 2

So, how do you know when to shift? A few key signals indicate that Level 1 is no longer the right tool for the job:

▸ You find yourselves circling the same points without new insights.
▸ One or both of you feel misunderstood or unheard, even after attempts to clarify.
▸ Emotions are rising, and the conversation starts feeling stuck, frustrating, or overwhelming.
▸ The discussion keeps expanding to include multiple issues rather than focusing on one.

Recognizing these clues allows you to pivot as a team. You can name the shift by saying, "I feel like we're getting stuck. Let's go to Level 2." This avoids the frustration of repeating the same points and sets the stage for a more intentional conversation.

The Three Level 2 Prompts

At this point, you transition into a more structured process using the three core prompts that define a Level 2 Wholehearted Conversation.

1. **How I see this the same...** This is where you look for agreement on two things: the facts ("I agree I was late") and the feelings ("I agree that neither of us wants you to feel unimportant"). (Example: "How I see this the same is that we both agree we feel disconnected lately - and neither of us wants that.")

2. **How I see this differently...** (Example: "How I see this differently is that I make up that you pull away when you feel like I'm pressuring you.")

3. **Sharing this feels...** (Example: "Sharing this feels anxiety-provoking, and I don't want to argue.")

Each partner takes turns, sharing one point at a time using the provided prompts, while the other reflects back what they heard, not to defend or fix, but simply to confirm understanding.

When sharing, always include the full prompt. This helps you stay anchored in the purpose of your message and gives your partner a clear reminder of what to reflect back. The prompt acts like a guidepost, helping both of you stay grounded in the process as you work toward clarity and connection.

"Being understood is the most powerful form of connection."

- SUE JOHNSON

CHAPTER 17
LEVEL 2
Narrowing the Focus

Welcome to Level 2. This is where we "handle the fire."

You've completed the preparation (Chapter 12), learned the Rules for the Road (Chapter 13), and become mindful of your non-verbals (Chapter 14). Now you are sitting down to talk, and the emotional intensity is already at a 4 or higher on the Scale of Distress (Chapter 11).

A Level 1 conversation won't be enough. You need more structure. You need the Table.

The Table is a symbolic, shared space where you will place one issue at a time. Its purpose is not to prove who's right, but to sort and untangle your different perspectives without overwhelm, so you can find the heart of the matter.

The Level 2 Process: Step-by-Step

All Level 2 conversations begin with the Level 1 No-Fault Formula. This is how you place the first topic on the Table.

Step 1: The Level 1 Entry (The No-Fault Formula)

The Sender (who has already gotten consent per Chapter 12) initiates the topic with the No-Fault Formula.

▶ **Sender:** "When we're sitting together in the evening and you're on your phone, I feel lonely, and the story I make up is that I'm not interesting or important to you."

Step 2: The Level 1 Cycle (Reflect & Confirm)

The Receiver reflects, and the Sender confirms. This is the basic loop you've already learned.

▶ **Receiver:** "What I hear you saying is that when I'm on my phone in the evening, you feel lonely, and it makes you wonder if you're important to me. Did I get it?"

▶ **Sender:** "Yes, you got it."

▶ **Receiver:** "Is there more on that point?"
Sender: "No, that's it."

Step 3: The Level 2 Pivot (The "0-10 Scale" Check-In)

Both Partners State

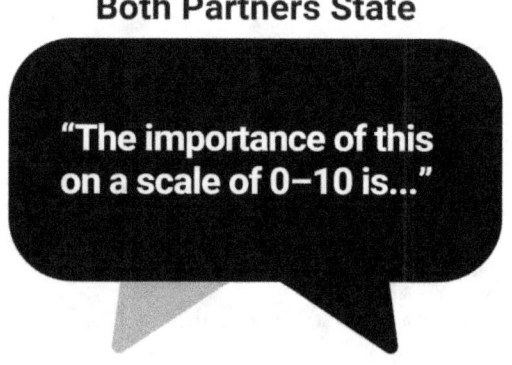

"The importance of this on a scale of 0–10 is..."

Before you dive deeper, you must take the temperature. The Receiver (who is about to become the New Sender) checks in. This check-in protects you from talking past each other. Two people can be discussing the same situation but living entirely different emotional realities. The scale helps you discover that before you step any further into the conversation.

▶ **Receiver (now New Sender):** "Before I respond, the importance of this topic to me, on a scale of 0-10, is a 3. It bothered me, but it's not a huge deal."

▶ **Sender (now New Receiver):** "For me, it's an 8. It's been happening a lot, and it's really hurting."

This simple check-in just revealed everything. The issue is a big deal (an 8) and needs the full Level 2 process. If both partners had said "3," you could have resolved it quickly and moved on. Because one person is an 8, you must proceed.

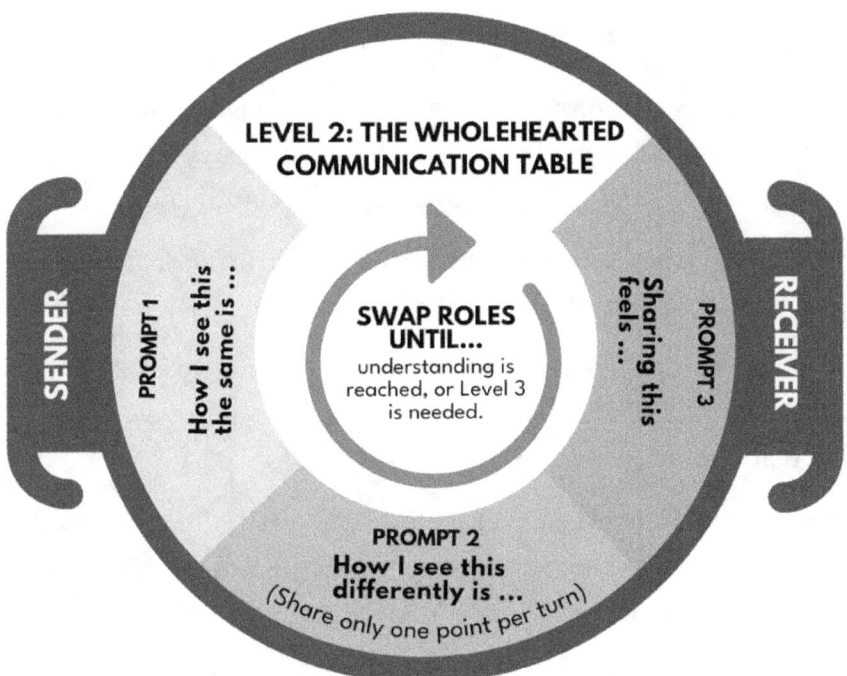

Step 4: The Level 2 "Sorting" (The Three Prompts)

Now, the *real* Level 2 process begins. The New Sender (the one who just gave their "3") doesn't just share their story. They use the three Table prompts to sort the issue.

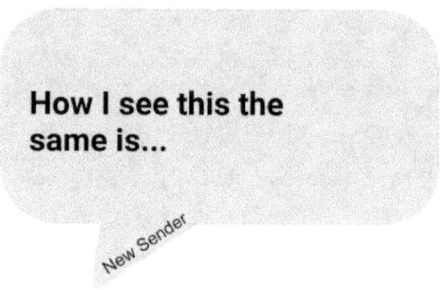

Prompt 1: "How I see this the same is..."

Conflict has a way of zooming in on differences. This prompt asks you to zoom out instead. It reminds you that you are on the same team and that the first job is to stand with your partner, not against them.

When your partner shares a hurt, they are really asking: Can you see what I am feeling, and can you stay with me long enough for me to feel less alone in it?

You look for the pain point they are naming and let them know you don't want them to feel that pain. It is the simplest and most powerful way to show that you are on the same side.

There are two places where you can find agreement. You can agree with the facts they shared, and you can agree with the feelings they are experiencing. Finding some agreement with both is ideal.

Agreeing with a feeling is not the same as confessing an intention to hurt them. You are not saying, "I meant to do that." You are saying, "I see that you are hurting, and I agree that neither of us wants you to feel this way." Aligning in this way softens the entire conversation.

▶ **New Sender:** "How I see this the same is that I do not want you to feel lonely or question your importance to me (feelings), and I agree I have been on my phone a lot (facts)."

This is the moment the conversation becomes one conversation again.

Prompt 2: "How I see this differently is..."

Introducing a different perspective can feel risky, especially if you fear it will make things worse. This prompt gives you a safe and structured way to share your experience without pulling away from your partner.

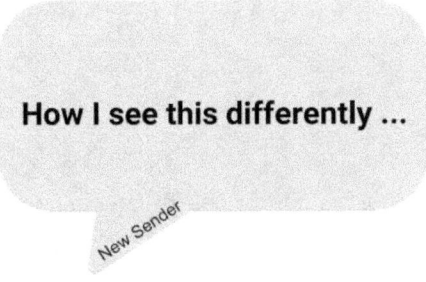

Once you have stood next to your partner and shown them that you see the same pain point and the same facts they have put on the table, you are ready for the pivot. This is where you begin to gently introduce your own perspective.

Think of it as changing the camera angle, not changing the story. You are not correcting your partner. You are not defending yourself. You are simply adding the part of the picture that you can see, and they cannot.

This step works best when you move slowly and remember that your goal is clarity, not victory. You are giving your partner access to your internal world without asking them to abandon their own.

A helpful way to think about it is this.

▶ Prompt 1 **(How I see it the same is)** says, "I am with you."

> ▶ Prompt 2 **(How I see it differently is)** says, "Here is where my experience takes a different turn."

When you share the difference, keep it rooted in your own thoughts, experiences, and intentions. Speak from the inside out instead of the outside in. This keeps you from drifting into blame or accusation.

For example, instead of saying, "You are exaggerating," or "You always think the worst of me," try offering something that is true and specific to you.

You might say:

"How I see this differently is that when I am on my phone, I am usually decompressing from the day, not trying to disconnect from you."

or

"How I see this differently is that I did not realize how often I was doing it. From my side, it felt occasional rather than constant."

Both of these statements add perspective without denying the other person's experience or pain. They widen the conversation instead of shutting it down.

Think of this prompt as opening a window, not closing a door. You and your partner are still talking about the same feelings, the same facts. Now you are simply adding your view so that together, you can build a fuller, more honest picture of what happened.

This is the heart of Level 2 communication. You begin with alignment, then you gently introduce difference, and the two of you create understanding in the space where those two truths meet.

> ▶ **New Sender:** "How I see this differently is that when I'm on my phone, I don't see it as taking away from our connection. I'm usually just decompressing from work, not trying to ignore you."

Prompt 3: "Sharing this feels…"

This is the vulnerability step. It names the emotion *of the conversation itself*.

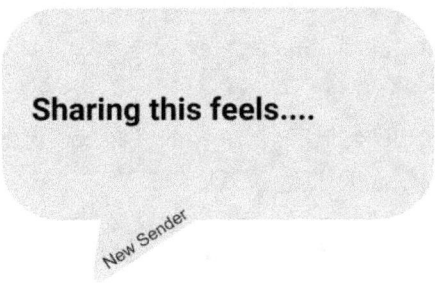

Prompt 3 is optional after the first round, and its purpose is simple. It helps you pause and name the emotion you are experiencing as you speak. Many people move quickly into logic or problem-solving, and this prompt brings you back to the emotional center of the conversation.

It is not meant to be dramatic or heavy. It is simply a tool to help you access your emotions as you speak.

For some couples, naming feelings comes naturally and becomes woven into their "same" and "different" sharing without much effort. For others, especially those who lean more toward analysis or self-protection, this prompt is the reminder that emotions belong in the conversation too.

You might say:

"Sharing this feels tender."

or
"Sharing this feels uncomfortable but important."

or
"Sharing this feels hopeful."

By naming how it feels to speak your truth, you help your partner understand not just the content of what you are saying, but the emotional experience behind it. It creates a softer, more connected tone and helps both people stay grounded in themselves instead of slipping into defensiveness.

Again, this prompt is optional after the initial round. Use it whenever it helps you access your emotions or stay connected to your partner. Over time, many couples find that this kind of emotional naming becomes second nature, naturally folding into their "same" and "different" sharing without needing a dedicated step.

Prompt 3 simply keeps the heart in the conversation, right alongside the facts and perspectives.

> ▶ **New Sender:** "Sharing this feels a little surprising because I didn't realize how much it affected you, and I'm anxious I'm failing you."

Step 5: The Level 2 Cycle (Reflect, Validate, Continue)

Once the New Sender has shared their three prompts, the New Receiver reflects back what they heard. The reflection is not a test of memory. It is simply a way to show, "I was with you, and I understood." That sense of being understood is what allows the conversation to move forward.

As the Receiver, you can reflect after each individual share, or, if you have a strong memory for details, you can hold the full set and reflect all three prompts at once. When you are first learning this process, it is usually best to reflect one share at a time. It keeps the pace slow and prevents overwhelm. As you become more comfortable, you can experiment with how much you can hold before reflecting. The only measure that matters is whether your partner feels heard and settled enough to continue.

Here is what a full reflection sounds like:

> ▶ **New Receiver:** "What I hear you saying is that you see it the same in that we both want to feel connected. You see it differently because

for you, being on your phone is a way to decompress, not to ignore me. And sharing this feels surprising and makes you anxious. Did I get all of that?"

▶ **New Sender:** "Yes, you got it."

Prompt 3 ("Sharing this feels...") is required the first time you speak in Level 2 because it helps anchor you emotionally. After that, it becomes optional. Use it anytime it helps you stay grounded or connected, and skip it when your emotions are naturally woven into your "same" and "different" sharing.

After the reflection, roles switch. The New Receiver becomes the New Sender and uses the three prompts in response to what they just heard. This creates a steady rhythm:

→ **Same**
→ **Different**
→ **Feels**
→ **Reflect**
→ **Switch.**

This cycle continues until both partners feel the topic is fully understood, not solved or fixed. When both people feel seen, heard, and settled, Level 2 has done its job.

Step 6: Identify the Outcome (Agreement vs. Gridlock)

Once you have sorted the issue together, you will land in one of two places.

1. A Full Agreement is Reached

The conversation leads to a resolution where both partners feel understood and find common ground.

> **Sam:** "I see now how much this impacts you. What if I put my phone away for the first 30 minutes when I get home?"

Alex: "That would mean a lot. And I can try to check in with the No-Fault Formula instead of letting my 'story' build up."

At this point, the issue is resolved and taken off the Table.

2. A Perpetual Issue Emerges (Gridlock)

This is the most critical concept for long-term relationships. Agreement is not the goal. Understanding is.

Dr. John Gottman's research shows that 69 percent of conflict in stable long-term relationships is perpetual. These are ongoing differences rooted in core values or personality traits that will never be "solved."

This means most of what you struggle with will not disappear, but it can become easier, softer, and far less painful once you truly understand each other's internal experience.

A *perpetual issue* becomes *gridlocked* when the conversation leads to shutdown, resentment, and hopelessness.

Here is an example from my own relationship. My wife and I have a perpetual issue around gifting. I love showing affection through gifts. She grew up with financial insecurity, so my spending can feel like a threat. For years, this was gridlocked. We were not fighting about gifts. We were wrestling with two different needs: my need to show love by giving, and her need to feel safe.

We will never fully agree on this. In fact, that is not even the goal. But it is no longer gridlocked. Through this process, we have learned what this issue represents for each of us. I understand her fear. She understands my love. We still see it differently, but the difference no longer divides us. That understanding has made all the difference.

Step 7: The Closing Ritual

Once you have cleared the Table or sorted everything down to the core perpetual issue, you close the conversation with intention.

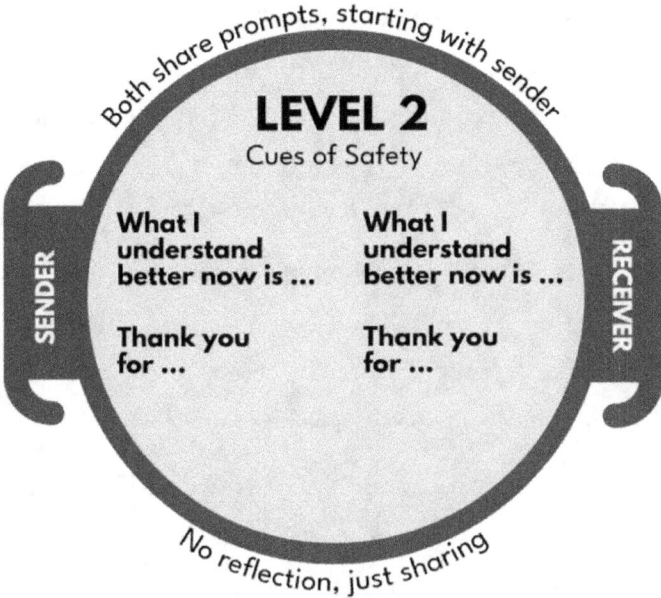

This is the shift back into cues of safety. Each partner takes a turn completing two prompts. There is no reflection during this step.

▶ **"What I understand better now is..."**

▶ **"Thank you for..."**

> **Alex:** "What I understand better now is that your phone use isn't always about disconnecting; it's sometimes just a habit. Thank you for really hearing me and for wanting to find a balance with me."

> **Sam:** "What I understand better now is how much this impacts you and how important it is for you to feel prioritized. Thank you for sharing your feelings and helping me see this from your perspective."

This is not a time to add "one last thought." The goal is closure. After a tense conversation, let it be closed. Shift your focus back to connection: take a walk, hug, or just sit quietly together.

Rules for the Level 2 Road (The Toolkit)

Level 2 works best when you have a few additional tools to stay steady. These help you navigate common obstacles without losing the connection you're building. As you use this process, you will get stuck. These tools help you stay grounded, connected, and on track.

Tool 1: Why Facts Alone Don't Resolve Conflict

Many disagreements get stuck because you remember things differently. You replay the details, trying to prove whose version is correct. But pushing for factual agreement often creates more distance.

> **Before (Debating Facts):** "I sent you a text!" "No, you didn't, I never got it!"

> **After (Shifting to Feelings):** "I can see that not getting a response made you feel ignored. That makes sense. I would feel the same way if I thought you saw my message and didn't answer."

When you stop debating details and start naming emotions, the conversation softens. The goal is not to win the facts. The goal is to understand the impact.

Tool 2: Beware of "Story-Blaming"

One of the sneakier troublemakers in communication occurs when you convince yourself you already know what your partner meant, felt, or intended. Your mind fills in the blank, fast and convincingly. The problem is that it is often wrong.

This is story-blaming.

Story-blaming is what happens when your imagination gets ahead of the facts. You take a fear or an old hurt, mix it with a little guesswork, and hand it to your partner as if you have uncovered the truth. They get blindsided and you get defensive.

Now you are arguing about a story that may not have happened at all.

A few examples, just to keep us honest:

▸ Your partner shifts slightly during a hug, and your mind announces, "Well, that is it. They are no longer attracted to me."

▸ They forget to text back, and the headline becomes, "You do not care about me."

▸ They sigh after a long day, and the internal narrator says, "You are upset with me."

These stories may feel true. But unless you verify them using the No-Fault Formula ("…and the story I make up is…"), sharing them will feel like an accusation or criticism.

Tool 3: Name the Dance

When you feel yourselves getting stuck in a familiar loop, name the dance.

▸ Pursue / Withdraw: One partner (the Bumblebee) presses, the other (the Turtle) retreats..

▸ Blame / Defend: One partner criticizes, the other justifies.

Naming the dance by saying, "I think we are in our criticize and defend pattern," creates just enough space to step out of it. Naming the dance helps both partners shift from reacting to observing, which softens the nervous system and interrupts the pattern.

Tool 4: Level 2 "Boosters"

These are small upgrades that deepen understanding.

▸ **Add "Because…"**
Don't just say "I feel hurt."
Say, "I feel hurt *because* I value our connection so much."

▶ **"Two-Hand Communication"**

Share two competing truths at once.

"On one hand, I'm afraid to bring this up because I don't want to fight. On the other hand, I'm feeling so lonely, I knew I had to say something."

What If That Shift Doesn't Happen?

Sometimes, even after a full Level 2 conversation, you still feel tension or disconnection. Before assuming you need to go deeper, pause and ask yourself two questions.

> **First:** Do we both feel heard and understood, even if we haven't agreed? If the answer is yes, Level 2 has done its job. Understanding, not agreement, is the goal. You can close the conversation with the Closing Ritual and let the issue rest. It may still be unresolved, but it is no longer stuck.

> **Second:** Does the pain feel bigger than the topic itself? If one or both of you keeps returning to a deeper hurt that the sorting process can't quite reach, that is your signal. You are no longer sorting the issue. You are brushing up against the wounds beneath it.

That is the territory of Level 3.

> **Say:** "I appreciate us talking through this. I can tell we've reached the end of what this level can do. I think this might be a Level 3 conversation."

Whether the issue is resolvable or perpetual, Level 2 will always bring you to a clearer understanding of what is happening between you. That understanding is what allows the two of you to reconnect, soften, and move forward together. In the next chapter, we will wade into the deeper waters that Level 2 often reveals.

LEVEL 2

WHOLEHEARTED COMMUNICATION

LEVEL 2

(S) SENDER   **(R) RECEIVER**

INTRO

Sender Starts Here

I'd like to talk about [topic], so that [goal/intention]. Is now a good time?

Yes or No. If no, propose and initiate an alternate time to talk within 24 hours.

(S)(R) Both state aloud  "I agree to stay on script, seek to understand, remain emotionally regulated, and I'm able to hold your hand."

LEVEL 1

No Fault Formula
When [facts/not stories], I feel [feeling word], and The story I make up is...

Correct/Clarify/Confirm
Yes, you got it.
No, you forgot...
What I meant was...

Fact Check
What I hear you saying ...
Did I get it?
Is there more on that point?

Once confirmed, both state importance. ↘

(S)(R) "The importance of this on a scale of 0-10 is ..."

LEVEL 2

Fact Check
What I hear you saying ...
Did I get it?
Is there more on that point?

Receiver Starts Here

How I see this the same is ...
How I see this differently is ...
Sharing this feels ...

⇄ **Correct/Clarify/Confirm**

Swap roles until you either see things the same or have identified the core of your differences. If still unresolved, proceed to Level 3, if resolved, skip to Cues of Safety.

CUES OF SAFETY

Once each shares above prompts, alternate sharing these without reflection:
What I understand better now is ...
Thank you for ...

(S)(R) When finished, exchange affection.

"Successful couples are simply those who keep trying."

- JOHN GOTTMAN

CHAPTER 18

LEVEL 3

Deepening Understanding and Healing

If Level 1 is about catching the smoke early, Level 2 is about sorting how you see the issue the same and differently. That sorting process helps contain and reduce the fire. Level 3 goes deeper, addressing the emotional wounds that keep feeding the wildfire.

At this level, you move beyond sorting the issue to healing the emotions beneath it. This is where the real heart-work happens. Level 3 conversations uncover the old wounds, fears, and unmet needs that make certain conflicts feel bigger than they "should."

Instead of asking, "What happened between us?" you ask, "What inside me is making this feel so painful?"

Why Certain Conflicts Feel So Big

Often, the pain we feel in a disagreement is about something our nervous system remembers from the past.

When a situation in your relationship *feels* like a past wound, your brain reacts as if it's happening all over again. You stop seeing your partner; instead, you react as if they were a parent who dismissed you or a friend who betrayed you.

According to Imago Relationship Theory, we are naturally drawn to partners who mirror both the strengths and struggles of our early caregivers and important others. This means the person you love most is also the one most likely to activate old wounds.

Level 3 conversations help you separate the past from the present. Without this separation, your old pain will piggyback on what's happening today.

How Level 3 Conversations Work

This is the most structured conversation. You transition to Level 3 when you've finished Level 2 but still feel stuck, disconnected, or in the grip of a gridlocked issue.

This process is broken into two distinct phases:

▶ **Phase 1:** The Healing Prompts (Prompts 1-6)
▶ **Phase 2:** The Closing Ritual (Prompts 7-8)

Phase 1: The Healing Prompts

Step 1: The Sender Shares (Prompts 1-6) The Sender begins and completes all six of the Healing Prompts below. After *each* prompt, the Receiver's only job is to mirror.

▶ **Sender:** (Shares Prompt 1: "What hurts most...")
Receiver: (Mirrors: "What I hear you saying is... Did I get it?")

▶ **Sender:** (Confirms, then shares Prompt 2: "What I'm afraid of...")
Receiver (Mirrors: "What I hear you saying is... Did I get it?")... and so on, until all six prompts are shared and mirrored.

Step 2: Switch Roles Once the Sender has completed all six prompts, you switch roles. The original Receiver now becomes the new Sender and completes the same six *Healing Prompts* (1–6), with their partner mirroring after each prompt using the same script.

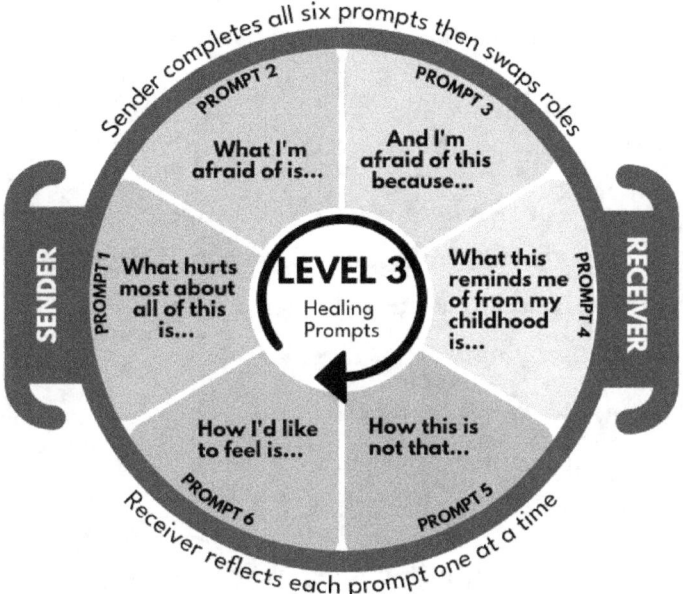

The Six Healing Prompts

1. What hurts most about all of this is... This is where we name the core feeling we're experiencing. Often, what hurts most is less about the topic and more about the dynamic it creates. There's no "right" answer here; it's what feels true to you.

If "hurt" doesn't feel like the right word, you can use "What's painful about this is..." instead. The goal is to uncover the vulnerability, the thing that makes this matter to you.

▶ **Example:** "What hurts me most is feeling like my opinion doesn't matter to you. When you made that decision without talking to me, I felt unimportant."

2. What I'm afraid of is... When you reflect on this situation, what worries come to mind? Maybe it's a fear of not mattering, of not being trusted, or of not being enough. Naming it helps bring your deeper fears to light and invites your partner to see the tender, human side of your reaction.

> ▶ **Example:** "I'm afraid this means we're growing apart and that I'll lose the connection we've worked so hard to build."

3. And I'm afraid of this because... This prompt invites us to dig a little deeper. Why does this fear hold so much weight? If you're afraid of not being trusted, what does that mean to you? This is the time to articulate what's at the heart of your worry.

> ▶ **Example:** "I'm afraid of this because I've felt invisible in past relationships, and that was always the beginning of the end. I'm scared that might happen again."

4. What this reminds me of from my childhood is... This is where we connect our current *feelings* to past experiences. The memory that surfaces might not be literal; it might be a time when you felt a similar *emotion* (mistrusted, doubted, rejected).

Sometimes, unrelated or "random" memories will pop into your mind. Don't dismiss them. Share them. These instances often give valuable insights. By bringing old wounds to light, we make it easier for our partner to feel compassion for us.

> ▶ **Example:** "This reminds me of how I felt when my parents never asked for my opinion about anything growing up. I felt like my voice didn't matter, and that feeling is showing up again now."

5. How this is not that... This is the critical step that separates the past from the present. It's about grounding ourselves in the now, and recognizing how this situation is different. This step helps us disconnect our present experience and emotions from the influence of old wounds.

▶ **Example:** "I know this is not that because I am an adult, not a child, and you are my partner. Furthermore, you've shown me how much you value our relationship. You were stressed when you made that decision, and I know it wasn't meant to hurt me."

6. How I'd like to feel is... This is the forward-looking prompt. It names the core need or the desired emotional state. It bridges the past with the future, giving your partner a clear and positive understanding of what you're longing for.

▶ **Example:** "How I'd like to feel is secure, prioritized, and like we're a team."

Phase 2: The Closing Ritual

Step 3: Close the Conversation (Prompts 7-8) *After* both partners have completed Phase 1 (all six prompts), you move into the final closing ritual together.

For these two prompts, the original Sender goes first. The focus shifts from reflection to receiving. These are not prompts you mirror back. They are meant to help each partner integrate what they learned and end the conversation with warmth and steadiness.

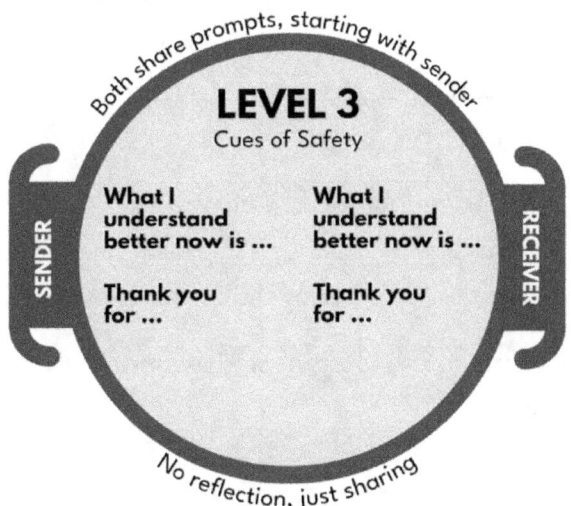

7. What I understand better now is... This prompt helps you name the insight or clarity you gained from the conversation.

> ▸ **Example (Sender):** "What I understand better now is that my reaction was super-charged by that old feeling of being invisible, not just from the decision you made. And I also understand better *your* fear of being overwhelmed."

8. Thank you for... This ends the conversation with gratitude and acknowledgment.

> ▸ **Example (Sender):** "Thank you for listening so patiently. I know it's not easy to hear, but I feel so grateful for how much you care."

After the original Sender shares both prompts, the Receiver simply listens. No reflection. No clarifying questions. No correcting the details. When the Sender is finished, the partners switch positions and the new Sender shares their two closing prompts.

This is not the time to fix, explain, or tidy things up. It's time to let understanding settle.

If Your Partner's Understanding Doesn't Feel Accurate

There will be times when your partner's "What I understand better now" does not feel accurate to you. They may misunderstand part of your story or emphasize something that feels off.

This is not the time to correct them. The purpose of these final prompts is to help your nervous system settle. This step is about closure. If you correct your partner here, you risk reactivating the conversation you just completed.

Instead, use a gentle acknowledgment that honors the effort without reopening the story.

For example:

- ▶ "Thank you. I appreciate your effort to understand me, and it's okay that we see some parts differently right now."
- ▶ "Thank you for sharing what makes sense to you. Some parts still feel different for me, and we can come back to those later if needed."
- ▶ "Thank you. I hear what you're taking from this, and I appreciate your willingness to stay in it with me."

If something feels important enough to revisit, you can bring it into a future Wholehearted Communication cycle. Just not here.

If You Do Not Experience a Deeper Understanding

Sometimes, despite your best efforts, you might reach the end of the conversation and realize you're still unable to see things the same way or gain a deeper understanding of your partner's experience.

When this happens, it's often a sign that the pain around this topic is too overwhelming to allow your heart to open fully.

We can only approach conversations from one of two places: connection or self-protection. Connection is open-hearted and curious. Self-protection is focused on staying safe. We can't do both at the same time.

This doesn't mean the conversation failed. It means the pain around this topic may be too intense to work through without outside support.

If, after multiple sincere attempts, one or both of you still feels stuck, it may be time to seek outside help. A skilled couples counselor, therapist, or coach can help slow things down, hold the emotional weight, and guide you toward healing.

Reaching out for support isn't failure. It's a commitment to your relationship.

A Final Word on Level 3

As with all three Levels, Level 3 conversations are about feelings, not fixes. They are designed to create understanding, repair, and emotional closeness.

As couples have more Level 3 conversations, they begin to understand each other's emotional landscape.

What's happening on the surface starts to make more sense when you can see what's happening underneath. The words and behaviors you experience in daily interactions are often shaped by things that never get said out loud.

As time passes, patterns start to take shape. Not every conflict reveals a new wound. Many couples discover they are bumping into the same few tender places again and again. The context may change. The topic may look different. But underneath, it's often the same wound showing up in different situations.

Recognizing this changes how couples relate to conflict. Instead of treating each disagreement as a new problem to solve, they begin to see it as another opportunity to understand something familiar more deeply.

For example, one couple I worked with kept arguing about very different things.

One week it was about their partner working late. Another week it was about plans changing at the last minute. Another time it was about one partner seeming distracted during dinner. Each conversation sounded different on the surface, and each one felt urgent in its own way.

A Level 3 conversation helps expose the recurring themes in our conflicts. By exploring times you've felt this way before, you can uncover old hurts that may keep popping up and super-charging the pain you're feeling today.

For one partner, each of these instances touched the same wound: *I don't matter enough to be prioritized.* When a text went unanswered, when plans shifted, when attention drifted, the body reacted as if something threatening was happening.

For the other partner, the same situations activated a different wound: *I'm never enough and I'm always doing something wrong.* Each complaint landed as proof of failure, even when no blame was intended.

They weren't fighting about phones, schedules, or dinner conversations. They were pressing against the same two wounds over and over, just dressed up in different circumstances.

Once they could see that, the conversations changed. Not because the issues disappeared, but because the meaning underneath them was finally visible. Instead of arguing about the details of each situation, they began responding to the fear and vulnerability driving them.

That shift didn't fix everything overnight. But it created understanding. And understanding made room for repair, compassion, and closeness.

For some couples, after experiencing several Level 3 conversations, they find they only need to use them sparingly. For others, especially at the beginning, Level 3 may be essential for many conversations as long-standing wounds are unpacked. In those cases, Level 3 provides a container that supports healing in a focused and effective way.

This level of conversation asks for patience, and a willingness to sit with discomfort. It's even slower by design. And it works best when there's already enough safety and skill in place from Levels 1 and 2 to support it.

The goal of Level 3 is not resolution. It's recognition. It's being able to say, *This makes sense now*, and to feel your partner understand something important about you, even if nothing changes right away.

When couples can do that, conflict loses some of its charge. The wounds don't disappear, but they become known, familiar, and less reactive. Over time, that shared understanding often becomes one of the strongest sources of closeness in a relationship. This is where healing occurs.

Go at your own pace and use the Levels that best suit your needs.

Because Level 3 conversations are the most vulnerable of the three, they can leave couples feeling tender as they step back into everyday life. How you transition out of these conversations matters. That process is important enough to deserve its own chapter.

WHOLEHEARTED COMMUNICATION

LEVEL ❸ **LEVEL ❸**

S SENDER   **R RECEIVER**

INTRO

Sender Starts Here

I'd like to talk about <topic>, so that <goal/intention>. Is now a good time?

Yes or No. If no, propose and initiate an alternate time to talk within 24 hours.

S R (Both state aloud) ☚ "I agree to stay on script, seek to understand, remain emotionally regulated, and I'm able to hold your hand.

LEVEL 1

No Fault Formula
When [facts/not stories], I feel [feeling word], and The story I make up is...

Correct/Clarify/Confirm
Yes, you got it.
No, you forgot...
What I meant was...

Fact Check
What I hear you saying ...
Did I get it?
Is there more on that point?

Once confirmed, both state importance.

S R The importance of this on a scale of 0-10 is ...

LEVEL 2

Fact Check
What I hear you saying ...
Did I get it?
Is there more on that point?

Receiver Starts Here
How I see this the same is ...
How I see this differently is ...
Sharing this feels ...

Correct/Clarify/Confirm

*Swap roles until you either see things the same or have identified the core of your differences. If still unresolved, proceed to Level 3, if resolved, skip to Cues of Safety.

LEVEL 3

Sender Starts Here
What hurts most about all of this is...
What I'm afraid of is...
I'm afraid of this because...
What this reminds me of from my childhood is...
How this is not that...
How I'd like to feel is...

Correct/Clarify/Confirm

Sender completes all the prompts while the Receiver fact checks. Then, switch roles and repeat.

Fact Check
What I hear you saying ...
Did I get it?
Is there more on that point?

CUES OF SAFETY

Once each shares above prompts, alternate sharing these without reflection:
What I understand better now is ...
Thank you for ...

S R When finished, exchange affection.

"We are never
more fragile than
when we are reaching
for connection."

- SUE JOHNSON

CHAPTER 19

The Tender Zone

Even after a conversation seems finished, something can still linger. You might walk away thinking it's resolved, only to feel tension flare back up hours, or even days later. That's because conflict isn't a linear process and sometimes it leaves behind a residue.

This in-between space, after the hard conversation but before full reconnection, is what I call the Tender Zone.

This space is fragile and easy to miss. If you are not paying attention, it is often where the next rupture begins.

After engaging in Wholehearted Communication, you are both in a heightened emotional state. It's tender because the openness required to connect also leaves you more exposed. Your nervous system doesn't move at the speed of insight. Just because you had a good talk doesn't mean your body agrees. You might leave a conversation feeling open, but twenty minutes later, you're spiraling with doubt. That's your system doing its thing. And, this is called the Tender Zone.

If we skip past it, trying to rush back to normal, we miss the moment when real growth is possible. Rushing this part often backfires. How long you stay here varies. One person might need a few minutes to settle; another might need a day. The key is honoring that each person processes in their own time and keeping the connection warm while they do.

The Science of the Tender Zone

When you feel emotionally vulnerable, your nervous system's primary instinct is to self-protect. As Polyvagal Theory educator Deb Dana explains in her book, *Anchored*, this system is finely attuned to relational cues of safety and danger.

Her work teaches us that there are three aspects of your nervous system that you cannot control.

- **You cannot control what triggers you.** This has little to do with willpower and everything to do with history. Your nervous system has been trained by your life experiences.
- **You cannot control the intensity of your activation.** The deeper the original wound, the stronger the reaction. When a current hurt brushes against an old wound, the body responds as if the past pain is happening all over again.
- **You cannot control how long your nervous system takes to return to baseline.** Some people can reset in minutes, others in hours or days. There is no "right" timeline. Speed is not the measure of health.

What you *can* do is notice what is happening. You can stay curious about what you need. You can stay kind to yourself and your partner while you both find your way back to solid ground.

Genuine empathy is about seeing through your partner's lens, not your own. It is about honoring their nervous system like you hope they will honor yours.

How to Navigate the Tender Zone

In this fragile space, your nervous systems are infectious. This is emotional contagion. If one of you remains dysregulated, it can unintentionally pull the other back into a reactive state.

But the reverse is also true: calm, grounded energy can help regulate *both* of you. Here is how to tend to the connection.

1. Send Cues of Safety (Often Without Words) This is the most important strategy. In the Tender Zone, your nervous system is on high alert. It's listening for reassurance, but it's watching for safety. This is why non-verbal cues of safety are often more powerful than any words you can say.

A verbal reassurance like, "Don't worry, we're okay," can be easily undermined by a tense body or a flat tone. Your partner's nervous system will believe the non-verbal cue over the verbal one every time.

A *true* non-verbal cue is direct and speaks straight to the emotional brain. This is the foundation of co-regulation. A simple, gentle touch, a soft, reassuring tone, or just sitting close without pressure are all powerful ways to say, "I am with you." They are the most effective way to help each other feel safe again.

2. Prioritize Self-Regulation Your ability to steady yourself also matters. Pay attention to what helps you come back to center: a slow breath, stepping outside, or placing a hand over your heart. When you take care of your own nervous system, you protect the connection.

3. Use Clear, Open Communication This is a time when clarity helps. Let your partner know what you need.

> ▶ "I need a little quiet right now, but I feel close to you."
> ▶ "Would it be okay if we just sat together for a bit?" This lowers the chances of misunderstandings.

4. Offer Repair Attempts Things might still feel a bit off. That's okay. What matters is finding your way back. You might offer a check-in later ("How are you feeling now?") or simply say something kind that helps soften the tension. Repair doesn't need to be complicated; it just needs to be sincere.

5. Respect Each Other's Needs You and your partner might need different things to feel settled. One of you may want to talk it through. The other might need quiet or space. The important part is letting each other know what helps you feel safe. Respecting each other's differences is one of the most caring things you can do.

A Bridge Back to Each Other

Tending to your nervous system is an opportunity to pay attention to your body and what it is telling you. The more you understand your cues, the better you will notice your partner's, too. When both of you are willing to care for yourselves and support each other, your relationship becomes a safe place to land. And that is where connection grows.

The tender zone is a reminder that even with the best intentions, reconnecting takes courage and care. It is one thing to want to close the distance. It is another to know how to take the first steps without getting pulled back into old patterns.

Sometimes what we need most is just a little space. A place to catch our breath, get honest about what we are feeling, and find some steady ground before we reach for each other again.

To assist in this process, you can utilize the Self-Awareness Worksheet (see appendix). It is not about getting it perfect. It is about giving yourself the support you need to stay open when staying open feels hard. The Self-Awareness Worksheet helps you slow down, sort through what is really happening inside, and step into the conversation with more clarity, more compassion, and more hope.

It is a bridge. A way to move from disconnection back into dialogue, from frustration back into understanding. One small, wholehearted step at a time.

"Love is not a feeling but a practice, and it requires knowledge and effort."

- ERICH FROMM

CHAPTER 20

The Road to Connection

As we reach the end of this book, we come full circle. We've explored the gap between our intentions and our impact. We've given names to our "dances," the Turtles and Bumblebees, and learned to recognize the "smoke" before it becomes a "wildfire." We've sat at the Table to sort our issues, and we've learned to heal in the Tender Zone.

Wholehearted Communication is not a destination. It is a lifelong commitment. The tools and insights shared here are meant to be practiced, refined, and sometimes even stumbled through. This path is paved with vulnerability, curiosity, and the willingness to grow. And like any journey, it begins with the first step, and that step is yours.

Many couples describe the early stages of practicing these tools as messy. Old habits resurface quickly. Self-protection takes over before they realize what is happening. The scripts feel awkward, sometimes even robotic. Progress can feel inconsistent, like one step forward and two steps back.

Many couples experience this when they first begin practicing these tools. Each time they show up, try again, or choose vulnerability over self-protection, something slowly shifts. Connection deepens. Understanding grows.

So, what's your next step?

You don't have to have all the answers. I invite you to simply continue the practice. Notice when you're in the Tender Zone. Pause and ask yourself, "What am I feeling, and how can I express that with compassion?"

You've learned the patterns that shape your communication, and with this awareness comes the power to change. You will slip up, and that's okay. What matters is that each ineffective attempt is an opportunity to choose again.

Remember, relationships are not problems to be solved but opportunities to grow together. You have already taken the first step toward that growth. Keep showing up with intention, keep practicing empathy, and keep inviting each other to care. Even a failed attempt to use a script is a cue of safety because it tells your partner you are trying. The effort itself is a bid for connection.

At the end of the day, the goal in any relationship is to become the safest emotional home for one another. That home is built one interaction at a time, and the way your relationship feels will ebb and flow, mirroring how you care for one another's thoughts, feelings, fears, and dreams. This is the work of love, and Wholehearted Communication makes it possible.

ACKNOWLEDGMENTS

I thank my pops for teaching me the joy of effortless conversations, my mom for creating the safety to share anything, and my soul friend, Kirsten, for modeling vulnerable sharing for so many decades.

To my clients, participants of my Wholehearted Communication class, and our Adventures in Love tribe, thank you for believing in me and my work. Your feedback has been invaluable in shaping The Art of Wholehearted Communication.

Thanks also to the learning communities where I grew my skill set, Imago Theory, The Gottman Method, Emotionally Focused Therapy (EFT), Polyvagal Theory, and Nonviolent Communication. These theories, research, and insights have been instrumental in shaping the development of this approach to intimate communication.

Thank you, Cam, for your pure heart and for always leading with kindness. Thank you, Mitch, for putting everything you have into everything you do and for always making me laugh.

And to you, Kristen, my love, thank you for being exactly who you are. Your love has turned me right side up and inside out in all the best ways. This book reflects our work. Thank you for living it alongside me and creating the safest, most joyful emotional home for my heart.

APPENDIX

The charts, worksheets, and scripts reference in the book are collected here and organized by the chapter in which they appear.

CHAPTER 7: Self-Protection

Damaging Defenses and Opposite Action

What are your go-to defensive moves that could use some opposite actions? Below is an inventory of common damaging defenses and the opposite action for each.

Place a check mark next to the defensive instincts you identify with. Also, take note of the opposite action.

☐ **Acting Superior** (*"I know better than you..."*)
▶ **Opposite Action:** Acknowledge and invite: "I'm realizing I'm acting like I have all the answers. I'm sorry. Can you tell me how you see it? I really want to understand."

☐ **Avoiding the Conversation**
▶ **Opposite Action:** Lean in with courage: "I am tempted to avoid this, but I know it's important. I'm here. Let's talk."

☐ **Blaming**
▶ **Opposite Action:** Take responsibility for your part: "You're right. A big part of this is on me. I'm sorry for blaming you."

☐ **Bringing in Third Parties** (*"Well, my friend agrees with me..."*)
▶ **Opposite Action:** Keep it between the two of you: "It doesn't matter what my friend thinks. This is about us. Let's focus on what you and I are feeling."

☐ **Bringing Up the Past**

▶ **Opposite Action:** Stay in the present: "You're right, I'm bringing up old stuff. Let's stick to what's happening right now. I feel…"

☐ **Brushing It Off** (*"This isn't a big deal."*)

▶ **Opposite Action:** Honor your partner's feelings: "I can see this is really bothering you. I'm sorry for brushing it off. Tell me more."

☐ **Criticism**

▶ **Opposite Action:** Repair and use the No-Fault Formula: "That came out as a criticism, I'm sorry. Let me try again: I feel frustrated when this happens, and I'd love to find a way we can fix this together."

☐ **Deflecting Blame**

▶ **Opposite Action:** Own your part: "You're right. I'm making excuses. My part in this was [action], and I'm sorry for that."

☐ **Demanding Immediate Resolution**

▶ **Opposite Action:** Give space when needed: "I know I'm pushing for an answer right now. You're right. Let's take a 20-minute break and cool off first."

☐ **Dismissing Apologies**

▶ **Opposite Action:** Accept and appreciate the effort: "Thank you for saying that. I really appreciate it. I accept your apology."

☐ **Escalating Conflict**

▶ **Opposite Action:** Lower your intensity and stay focused: "I'm getting really worked up, and I don't want to fight. Can we slow down? I feel unheard, and I want to work through this."

☐ **Exaggerating** (*"You always...," "You never..."*)

▶ **Opposite Action:** Stay specific and repair: "I know I just said 'you always' and that's not fair. What I mean is that *today*, when [the specific fact] happened, I felt..."

☐ **Expecting Mind-Reading**

▶ **Opposite Action:** Clearly state your needs: "I realize I was expecting you to read my mind, which isn't fair. What I actually need is [specific need]."

☐ **Guilt-Tripping**

▶ **Opposite Action:** Express your feelings without manipulation: "I feel disappointed, and I want to discuss how we can approach this differently."

☐ **Interrupting**

▶ **Opposite Action:** Pause and listen fully: "I'm sorry, I just cut you off. Please finish your thought. I'm listening."

☐ **Making It a Competition** (*"I have it worse than you..."*)

▶ **Opposite Action:** Show empathy instead: "You're right. This isn't a competition of who's more stressed. It sounds like this is really hard for you. I'm sorry."

☐ **Minimizing Your Partner's Feelings**

▶ **Opposite Action:** Validate instead of dismissing: "You're right, that's me minimizing. I can see this is really important to you. Tell me more about how you're feeling."

☐ **Name-Calling**

▶ **Opposite Action:** Stay respectful and repair: "That was not okay for me to say. I'm sorry. I'm upset, but I will not call you names."

☐ **Over-Explaining/Justifying**

▶ **Opposite Action:** Acknowledge impact instead of defending: "You're right. I'm justifying my actions, but that's not what's important. I hear that what I did hurt you, and I am sorry for that."

☐ **Passive-Aggressiveness**

▶ **Opposite Action:** Use direct communication and repair: "I'm sorry, I was being passive-aggressive. What I'm really trying to say is that I feel..."

☐ **Raising Your Voice**

▶ **Opposite Action:** Soften your tone: "I'm raising my voice, and I don't want to. I'm going to take a breath. I'm upset, but I want to talk about this calmly."

☐ **Sarcasm/Mocking**

▶ **Opposite Action:** Repair and be direct: "That was sarcastic and uncalled for. I'm sorry. Let me say what I actually mean..."

☐ **Shaming Your Partner**

▶ **Opposite Action:** Repair and focus on the problem: "What I just said was meant to make you feel bad, and that's not okay. I'm sorry. The real issue for me is..."

☐ **Shutting Down the Conversation**

▶ **Opposite Action:** Keep the door open (use the "Healthy Pause"): "I feel myself shutting down. Can we please take 20 minutes? I promise I will come back and finish this."

☐ **Stonewalling** (Silent Treatment)

▶ **Opposite Action:** Communicate your need for space: "I know I'm being silent, and that's not fair. I'm feeling overwhelmed right now, and I need some time to process."

☐ **Threatening to Leave**

▶ **Opposite Action:** Instead of threatening, express the feeling: "I'm feeling overwhelmed, and my first instinct is to run. But I want to figure this out together. I just need a time out."

☐ **Turning the Conversation Around** (*"Well, you did it first..."*)

▶ **Opposite Action:** Stay accountable: "You're right. I'm turning this back on you. Let's focus on what you just said. I'm listening."

☐ **Withholding Affection**

▶ **Opposite Action:** Maintain connection (give a cue of safety): (Reaching for their hand) "I'm still upset, but I want you to know I love you. We're going to figure this out."

CHAPTER 17: Level 2, Narrowing the Focus
Level 2 Wholehearted Communication Conversation: Cheat Sheet

1. Set the Topic and Purpose
- **Sender:** "I'd like to talk about [topic], so that [goal/intention]. Is now a good time?"

2. Confirm Readiness
- **Receiver:**
  - If ready: "Yes"
  - If not: "No, but..." (propose a time within 24 hours)

3. Establish Intentions (Both Partners Say Aloud)
- "I agree to stay on script, seek to understand, remain emotionally regulated, and I'm able to hold your hand."

4. Open With No-Fault Formula
- **Sender:** "When you [fact], I feel [emotion], and the story I make up is [interpretation]."

5. Reflect and Confirm
- **Receiver:** "What I hear you saying is... Did I get it?"
- **Sender:** Confirms, clarifies, or corrects.

6. Check for More
- **Receiver:** "Is there more on this point?"

7. Calibrate Distress Level
- **Sender:** "On a scale of 1-10, my distress about this issue is a [number]."
- **Receiver:** "For me, my distress about this issue is a [number]." (This is not for debate, just for mutual understanding of the intensity.)

8. Explore The Table Prompts

- **Phase 1: Original Listener Responds**
  - **Listener (New Sender):**
    - "How I see this the same is..."
    - "How I see this differently is..."
    - "Sharing this feels..." (optional after first time)
  - **Sender (New Receiver):**
    - Reflects and asks: "Did I get it?"

- **Phase 2: Roles Switch Back**

  - **Sender (New Sender):**
    - "How I see this the same is..."
    - "How I see this differently is..."
    - "Sharing this feels..." (optional after first share)
  - **Receiver (New Receiver):**
    - Reflects and asks: "Did I get it?"

9. Continue Switching Roles (Repeat Step 8)

- Alternate turns using the three prompts.
- Stay with one point at a time until it's fully understood.

10. Close The Conversation: Cues Of Safety

- **Each Partner Says (No Reflection, Just Sharing)**
  - "What I understand better now is..."
  - "Thank you for..."
- When finished, exchange affection.

You will repeat Step 8, swapping roles multiple times, until you both share your thoughts and feelings and have been heard.

Level 2 Wholehearted Communication Self-Check List
Using the Checklist

In most cases, couples get caught in patterns of ineffective sharing due to dysregulation and not sticking to the script.

This checklist is a simple tool to see your progress and find your next step. It's not a scorecard. It's designed to help you pinpoint *exactly* where a conversation went off track. When you can identify whether it was due to dysregulation or a missed step in the script, you know what to work on next time.

You may discover the real issue wasn't the *topic* but a shared *pattern*. Recognizing this pattern is the first step to changing it.

As you reflect on your last Level 2 conversation, check off every win. Each checkmark shows progress.

Readiness & Grounding

- ☐ We each checked our emotional state before starting.
- ☐ We paused to rate the importance of the topic on a 0–10 scale.
- ☐ We shared our intentions aloud, including the statement:
    "I agree to stay on script, seek to understand, remain emotionally regulated, and I'm able to hold your hand."
- ☐ We briefly held hands or checked in physically before starting, and it felt comfortable.

Structure & Process

- ☐ The Sender clearly introduced one specific topic using the No-Fault Formula.
- ☐ The Receiver reflected back without defending, fixing, or correcting.
- ☐ The Sender confirmed or clarified until they said, "Yes, you got it."
- ☐ The Receiver asked, "Is there more?" before responding with their own view.

The Table Prompts Each partner used the three prompts, multiple times, taking turns to narrow the focus:

- ☐ "How I see this the same is..."
- ☐ "How I see this differently is..."
- ☐ "Sharing this feels..." (optional after first share)

Emotional Safety & Regulation

- ☐ We slowed the pace and didn't interrupt or talk over each other.
- ☐ We stayed emotionally grounded (or paused to regulate when needed).
- ☐ We stuck to one point at a time and didn't introduce new topics midstream.
- ☐ We stuck to the script exactly, and did not distract, redirect, interrupt, or ask each other questions during the conversation.
- ☐ We maintained neutral body language and did not use non-verbal communication as a way of communicating without words.

Connection & Resolution

- ☐ We focused on our inner experience, sharing what was going on within, instead of relying heavily on "what I make up about you," or the other's behavior.
- ☐ We closed with the two Cues of Safety:
  - "What I understand better now is..."
  - "Thank you for..."
- ☐ We did not reflect or correct what was shared in the final two prompts; we just listened.
- ☐ We did not rehash the conversation after it ended.
- ☐ We asked each other what we needed afterward to reset or reconnect.

When to Move from Level 2 to Level 3

Sometimes, a Level 2 conversation isn't enough, even with your best efforts. If you find yourselves repeating the same points without progress, or if emotions remain high, it's a sign that the conversation is hitting a deeper layer that requires emotional excavation rather than clarity and compromise.

Key Differences Between Level 2 and Level 3 Conversations:
Level 2 Conversations:

▶ Help clarify misunderstandings and prevent minor conflicts from escalating.

▶ Focus on staying present with structured prompts to explore similarities, differences, and emotions.

▶ Aim for mutual understanding, even if complete agreement isn't reached.

▶ Provide a solution-focused way to resolve immediate concerns.

Level 3 Conversations:

▶ Go deeper than the present issue, uncovering emotional wounds, unmet needs, or core values.

▶ Address issues that keep resurfacing, even after multiple discussions.

▶ Often feel more personal and identity-threatening, rather than situational.

▶ Require emotional excavation and vulnerability, not just structured dialogue.

▶ We exchanged affection as part of a closing ritual.

CHAPTER 18: Level 3, Deepening Understanding and Healing
Level 3 Wholehearted Communication Conversation Self-Check

Use this checklist after completing a Level 3 conversation. For each item you left unchecked, reflect on how you can do better next time. Once you practice enough, and you are able to check all of these boxes, you will experience effective, fail-proof communication.

Before the Conversation

- ☐ We both agreed this was a Level 3 conversation (not stuck in Level 2).
- ☐ We paused to ground ourselves emotionally before beginning.
- ☐ We committed to listen, reflect, stay curious, and not defend.

During the Conversation

- ☐ We followed all six Level 3 Healing Prompts in order.
- ☐ After each prompt, the Receiver mirrored and waited for confirmation/clarification/correction.
- ☐ We avoided offering advice or making it about our viewpoint while the other was sharing.
- ☐ Both partners completed all six prompts before moving to Cues of Safety.

After the Conversation

- ☐ We used the two Cues of Safety to close (without reflecting or correcting)
  - "What I understand better now is..."
  - "Thank you for..."
- ☐ We did not reflect or correct what was shared in the final two prompts; we just listened.
- ☐ We felt more emotionally connected or gained a greater understanding of each other once it was completed.

☐ If we still felt disconnected, we acknowledged it and agreed on what to do next.

Emotional Check-In

☐ We each felt genuinely seen and heard.

☐ We avoided interrupting each other.

☐ We asked to "empty" when we needed to reflect what we heard before continuing to listen.

☐ We did not ask questions, instead we shared our feelings and owned our stories.

☐ We noticed when past experiences were influencing our reactions.

☐ We responded to each other's vulnerability with care, not criticism.

☐ When finished, exchange affection.

CHAPTER 19: The Tender Zone
Self-Awareness Worksheet

Some conversations are harder than others. Maybe you have tried to work through something, and it keeps circling back. Maybe you leave a discussion feeling more disconnected than when you started. Maybe you are doing your best, but nothing seems to change. If that sounds familiar, this worksheet is for you.

The Self-Awareness Worksheet is a guided tool to help you pause, reflect, and get grounded before stepping into a tough conversation. It walks you through a clear process that helps you sort through what you are feeling, why it matters, and how to say it in a way that invites your partner in, instead of pushing them away.

This is about showing up with more self-awareness, more intention, and more capacity for connection.

As you move through the worksheet, you will begin to recognize your emotional triggers, the ways you self-protect, and the patterns that keep you stuck. The process helps you name what is happening inside of you so you can speak openly, clearly, honestly, and without blame.

Some couples use this when they feel stuck. Others use it as a regular practice to stay connected. Either way, the goal is the same: to create a safe and intentional space where both of you can be real with each other and move toward connection and, in some cases, repair.

You do not need to have all the answers. You just need a way back to each other. And this is a place to start.

Self-Awareness Worksheet (SAW)
A Step-by-Step Guide to Reconnecting

Copies of SAW are available online at:
https://www.lesbianloveadv.com/SAW

The SAW Method

This worksheet helps you slow down and *see* what happened inside you. You will reflect on the facts, the story, the sensations, the emotions, the need underneath, and the intention behind your actions.

In other words...
This is what I SAW.

STEP ONE: SELF-AWARENESS

Before starting the conversation, take time to reflect. This step allows you to clarify your thoughts, regulate your emotions, and create a more open and meaningful dialogue.

1. FACTS

Describe the event (only the facts).
On [date & time], what happened was...

2. TRIGGER

The exact moment I recall feeling activated was when... Describe the specific trigger, facial expression, comment, tone of voice, behavior, etc.)

3. THE STORY I MADE UP

The meaning I attached to this event was... (Select or describe what resonates most.)

- ☐ It felt unfair or hurtful
- ☐ It was different than what I expected or hoped for

☐ It surprised or confused me
☐ It felt threatening or unsafe
☐ It made me doubt myself
☐ Other:

Now describe the story you created to make sense of what happened. How did you interpret the facts? What did you assume or believe was happening?

4. PHYSICAL SENSATIONS

How my body experienced these feelings ... (Check all that apply.)

_____Blank mind   _____Lump in throat

_____Chest pressure   _____Muscle tension

_____Clenched jaw   _____Nausea

_____Difficulty swallowing   _____Neck tension

_____Dizziness   _____Numbness

_____Dry mouth   _____Queasy

_____Energy rush   _____Rapid breathing

_____Face tight   _____Shaking

_____Headache   _____Shallow breathing

_____Heavy feeling   _____Sweating

_____Hot face/neck   _____Weakness

_____Hyperventilating   _____Other:

_____Heart racing   _____

5. EMOTIONS

I feel ...(Choose a primary and secondary emotion.)

Primary Emotion (immediate emotional reaction):

_____

Secondary Emotion (feeling about the immediate emotional reaction):

_____

6. UNMET NEED

The unmet need (or needs) these emotions point to is...

7. SELF-PROTECTIVE URGE

When this happened, and these feelings arose, my strongest self-protective urge was to...

8. ACTION

How I responded to this urge was...

9. INTENTION

What I had intended my actions to achieve was...

10. OUTCOME

The actual outcome of my actions was...

11. RESONANCE

What this experience reminds me of from my childhood is...

12. THIS IS NOT THAT

How this situation is different from my childhood and past experiences is...

13. EMPATHY

When I put myself in my partner's shoes, I imagine they felt...

14. REDO

If I could go back in time and redo this, I would:

- ▶ Better align my actions with my true intentions by...
- ▶ Regulate my emotions before responding by...
- ▶ Adjust my words or tone to better communicate my needs without escalating the conflict by...
- ▶ Invite my partner into a co-regulation moment instead of reacting alone by...

15. RESPONSIBILITY

How I can take responsibility for meeting this unmet need more effectively is...

STEP TWO: THE CONVERSATION

Now that you have reflected on your story, feelings, goal, and needs, you're ready to engage in the conversation.

Guidelines for the Conversation

1. Ask your partner for a conversation about the event.
2. Explain your intention (redo, repair, reconnect).
3. Invite your partner to complete this worksheet beforehand if they would like.
4. Take turns. One partner shares a response; the other reflects back to confirm understanding.
5. Repeat for each prompt. Once all prompts are shared and reflected back, switch roles.

CONVERSATION PROMPTS

Complete these prompts separately before discussing. Use your answers from the Self-Awareness Worksheet above. (The numbers in brackets correspond to the worksheet question numbers.)

1. When [#1] happened, I felt [#5]
2. And inside my body, I was experiencing [#4].
3. The story I told myself was [#3].
4. When that happened, my strongest urge was to [#7].
5. And I responded by [#8].
6. My intention in that moment was to [#9].
7. But the actual outcome was [#10].
8. What this reminds me of from my childhood is [#11].
9. What I now understand is that this situation is different from my past because [#12].
10. When I imagine what this was like for you, I think you may have felt [#13].
11. The unmet need underneath my reaction was [#6].

12. If I had a do-over, I would [#14].

13. And, I can take responsibility for meeting this need more effectively by [#15].

Once you have finished each prompt, ask your partner to summarize what they heard you say.

What I hear you saying is ... Did I get it?

Before moving on, ask your partner to confirm, clarify, or correct.

▶ **Confirm:** "Yes, you got it." (Then proceed to the next prompt).

▶ **Clarify:** "You got everything except..." (Receiver restates clarification)

▶ **Correct:** "No, what I said/meant was..." (Receiver restates correction)

Once you've shared all prompts, invite your partner to do the same while you reflect back what you hear them saying. Ask your partner to confirm, clarify, or correct your understanding.

KEY INFLUENCES

Brown, Brené. *The Gifts of Imperfection: Let Go of Who You Think You're Supposed to Be and Embrace Who You Are.* Center City, MN: Hazelden, 2010.

Brown, Brené. *Daring Greatly: How the Courage to Be Vulnerable Transforms the Way We Live, Love, Parent, and Lead.* New York: Gotham Books, 2012.

Dana, Deb. Anchored: *How to Befriend Your Nervous System Using Polyvagal Theory. New York:* St. Martin's Essentials/Sounds True, 2021.

Gottman, John M., and Nan Silver. *The Seven Principles for Making Marriage Work.* New York: Harmony Books, 1999.

Gottman, John M. *The Science of Trust: Emotional Attunement for Couples.* New York: W. W. Norton & Company, 2011.

Hanh, Thich Nhat. *True Love: A Practice for Awakening the Heart. Boulder,* CO: Shambhala Publications, 2004.

Hendrix, Harville, and Helen LaKelly Hunt. *Getting the Love You Want: A Guide for Couples.* New York: Holt Paperbacks, 1988.

Johnson, Sue. *Hold Me Tight: Seven Conversations for a Lifetime of Love.* New York: Little, Brown and Company, 2008.

Levine, Amir, and Rachel Heller. *Attached: The New Science of Adult Attachment and How It Can Help You Find—and Keep—Love.* New York: TarcherPerigee, 2010.

Linehan, Marsha M. *DBT Skills Training Manual. 2nd ed.* New York: Guilford Press, 2015.

Menanno, Julie. *Secure Love: Create a Relationship That Lasts a Lifetime.* New York: Simon & Schuster, 2024.

Porges, Stephen W. *The Polyvagal Theory: Neurophysiological Foundations of Emotions, Attachment, Communication, and Self-Regulation*. New York: W. W. Norton & Company, 2011.

Porges, Stephen W. *Polyvagal Safety: Attachment, Communication, Self-Regulation*. 1st ed. New York, NY: W. W. Norton & Company, Inc., 2021.

Rosenberg, Marshall B. *Nonviolent Communication: A Language of Life*. 3rd ed. Encinitas, CA: PuddleDancer Press, 2015.

Van der Kolk, Bessel. *The Body Keeps the Score: Brain, Mind, and Body in the Healing of Trauma*. New York: Penguin Books, 2014.

Welwood, John. *Perfect Love, Imperfect Relationships: Healing the Wounds of the Heart*. Boulder, CO: Shambhala Publications, 2006.

ABOUT THE AUTHOR

Michele O'Mara, PhD, has spent nearly three decades helping couples stop spinning in the same old arguments and start creating lives that feel connected and real. A relationship coach, retreat leader, and author, she is certified in Imago Relationship Therapy, trained in all three levels of the Gottman Method, and experienced in Emotionally Focused Therapy. Michele also holds a PhD in Sexology.

Alongside her wife, Kristen, Michele leads destination retreats for lesbian couples who are ready to reconnect. When she's not guiding couples, she writes, adventures, travels, and enjoys everyday life with her favorite people.

Learn more at www.micheleomara.com